ENDORSEMENTS

In *A Touch From Heaven*, Neal Pylant tells a compelling saga filled with his family's struggle to triumph over deadly, demonic disease, terrifying generational and spiritual attacks, as well as their own doubts and fears. What would a family do when their beloved preschooler is diagnosed with untreatable cancer? Discover how God, faith, and a family's journey took them to the brink of despair and beyond. This may be the most amazing miracle story I have ever read!

DR. LARRY KEEFAUVER
Bestselling Author and International Speaker

A Touch From Heaven: A Little Boy's Story of Surgery, Heaven, and Healing gives a wonderful account of God's healing power, and it will greatly bless those who read it.

MARK RUTLAND, PH.D.
Author/Speaker and President of Oral Roberts University

When things are bad, we take comfort in the thought that they could always be worse. And when they are, we find hope in the thought that things are so bad they have to get better. Get ready for a taste of extreme faith! This excellent book portrays the Pylant family's real life experiences that go from the deepest despair to ultimate triumph when their only child was diagnosed with a life-threatening disease.

By sharing so honestly their day-to-day struggles, the reader will receive encouragement to face life's challenges with grace by understanding that no matter how hopeless their situation, with God all things are possible! God still works miracles! Christopher is a living testimony of His healing power. Neal, Carole, and Christopher fought a good fight and finished strong! This book will impact many lives for eternity.

DOTTI CASORIA
Trinity Broadcasting Network

God is using this emotionally gripping true story of faith, fortitude, and healing to confirm He is real. Heaven is real. Healing is real. This remarkable story has a wonderful ending that gave me increased hope and faith in our good God!

PATTI MILLER DUNHAM
Author of *I Saw Heaven!*

I remember the morning Neal and Carole walked through the doors of River of Life Church with their dying son. I can still see them clearly, standing at the altar with the look of both desperation and hope on their faces. God moved in such a powerful way that morning! Not only were their lives changed, but ours as well. After all these years, I still remember standing with them as we prayed for Christopher and cursed the root of the tumor and commanded it to die in the name of Jesus. The battle for Christopher's life escalated and the warfare was intense, but God came through for their family in a powerful way. I feel so humbled and blessed that I was chosen to be a part of such a wonderful miracle. God has opened a door for this powerful story to be shared with the world. I am convinced many lives will be changed as they read the account of the Pylant's tenacious faith in God.

PASTOR BOB WRIGHT
Harvest Family Church, Dallas, Texas

A TOUCH *from* HEAVEN

A Touch *from* Heaven

A Little Boy's Story of Surgery,

Heaven, and Healing

NEAL PYLANT

&

CHRISTOPHER PYLANT

DESTINY IMAGE® PUBLISHERS, INC.

P.O. Box 310, Shippensburg, PA 17257-0310

"Promoting Inspired Lives."

This book and all other Destiny Image, Revival Press, MercyPlace, Fresh Bread, Destiny Image Fiction, and Treasure House books are available at Christian bookstores and distributors worldwide.

For a U.S. bookstore nearest you, call 1-800-722-6774.

For more information on foreign distributors, call 717-532-3040.

Reach us on the Internet: www.destinyimage.com.

ISBN 13 TP: 978-0-7684-0327-5

ISBN 13 Ebook: 978-0-7684-8573-8

For Worldwide Distribution, Printed in the U.S.A.

1 2 3 4 5 6 7 8 / 17 16 15 14 13

DEDICATION

This book is dedicated to God, who gives life and life more abundantly.

ACKNOWLEDGMENTS

Many have asked me, "Why did you wait so long to write this book?" With each attempt to write the story, the doors of opportunity closed, oftentimes abruptly. And I came to realize who was closing those doors. As it was with the battle for Christopher's life, our prayers were answered in God's timing, not our own.

My deepest gratitude goes to all who lovingly supported Carole, Christopher, and me during our time of need and to those who encouraged and assisted me in writing our story.

To Larry Keefauver and Maureen Haner, many thanks for believing in our story and assisting me in the development of this manuscript.

To Ronda Ranalli, Acquisition Managing Editor with Destiny Image, who accepted this project, a mere thanks seems inadequate in light of your kindness, your willingness to listen, and your professionalism in guiding me, step by step, through the publishing process. For this I will be forever grateful.

Thanks to Destiny Image Publishers for giving me, a first-time author, the opportunity to share this extraordinary story with the world and to the team who worked diligently to produce such a beautiful book: Terri Meckes, Project Manager; Dominique Abney, Art Director; Darren Rettburg, for text layout; and Trena Oyler, Author Marketing Consultant, who helped me promote my book.

I want to especially express my heartfelt love and appreciation to my wonderful wife, Carole, for her support and encouragement and for her contribution in writing the manuscript. A special thanks to my son and co-author, Christopher, for sharing some of the most personal aspects of his life.

Last, but never least, I give all praise and honor to God, from whom all life is given. If we had not received a touch from heaven, this story would have never been told.

"You never know how much you really believe anything until its truth or falsehood becomes a matter of life and death to you."
—C.S. Lewis

"If all things are possible with God, then all things are possible to him who believes in Him."
—Corrie Ten Boom

CONTENTS

FOREWORD

Dr. Benjamin S. Carson, Sr., M.D.

A Touch From Heaven is a great description for this story of a family who faced indescribable discouragement in the face of a tumor at the base of their only child's brain, which appeared inoperable and did not appear to be survivable.

When I first met the Pylants and saw Christopher, I wondered what it was that they expected me to be able to do. I had reviewed the CAT scans and concurred with all the others that this was a tumor that involved the brain stem and encircled the major vessels and simply was not something that was going to respond in any significant way to an operation.

The Pylants listened politely to my explanations, but then insisted that God would heal their son and that I would be involved. I consulted with some of the neuroradiologists and we did an MRI, which was a new technology at the time, but unfortunately the results were the same. There is no question that we had seen tumors of this type previously, and we knew what the outcomes were likely to be. Nevertheless, the Pylants still continued to impress me with their tenacious faith that God would somehow heal their son.

Some of my colleagues were quite skeptical and I must say that I could not blame them, although I certainly shared a great deal of faith in God with the Pylants. At the end of Christopher's first operation, I was greatly saddened to see that this appeared to be a highly malignant lesion. It turned out that after the second surgery, Christopher made a remarkable recovery and one of the oncologists, an atheist, stated that he was now a believer.

For those who read this wonderful book, I believe their lives will be touched by this remarkable journey of faith.

BENJAMIN S. CARSON, SR., M.D.
The Benjamin S. Carson, Sr., M.D. and Dr. Evelyn Spiro,
R.N. Professor of Pediatric Neurosurgery
Director of Pediatric Neurosurgery
Professor of Neurological Surgery, Oncology,
Plastic Surgery, and Pediatrics
Johns Hopkins Medical Institutions

FOREWORD

Margaret English-de Alminana, Ph.D.

The valley of the shadow of death is a place most of us visit just once, and very few come back to describe their arduous trek through that valley. Behind those shadows are places and discoveries that few of us have understood or wrestled with. Christopher, Carole, and Neal Pylant's journey along that path may seem a little strange to those who have never walked that way. Their descriptions of the looming challenges that cast those shadows may stretch us a little, but their story and joyful success is a wonder we can all embrace.

Many years ago, I too experienced a dramatic miracle in my own body following a devastating car accident. Having walked that path myself, I know through my own personal experience that the Pylant's miracle is real, and their battle with unseen forces that stand just beyond the veil of this life is equally compelling. Most of us meet Christ as Savior, but fewer of us meet Him as Healer. In my own life the two were so closely related that I never have been able to separate them. I doubt that Neal, Carole, and Christopher can either. For once that Divine Hand has touched you, once your life has been utterly transformed by the certainty of divine and miraculous power and love, you are never quite the same again. From that time forward the Healer, Savior, Lover, and Redeemer can no longer be compartmentalized or categorized in our limited human perception. From that time forward, these aspects of Christ become fused together into an expression or manifestation of His pure and perfect love.

Healing evangelist Kathryn Kuhlman, well known for services wherein hundreds and sometimes thousands claimed to have been dramatically touched and miraculously and instantaneously healed, described her theological understanding of healing in much the same way. She saw healing, miracles, salvation, and redemption as an expression of Christ's *agape* love. She said, "Love is something you do. The very last thing He did before He went away was to give the Holy Spirit to the church. You can't love, without giving. That's the reason He gave the church the greatest possible gift; there is no greater gift than the person who had been so faithful…the one who had not failed Him. You shall receive power after that the Holy Ghost comes upon you."[1]

That wonderful power and gracious deliverance is in itself a foretaste and expression of God's perfect love. Those of us so uniquely blessed by the miraculous healing touch of God often sense that we've entered briefly beyond the veil of this life to a place where perfect love reigns freely in the person and character of Jesus Christ.

In reading this wonderful story of the miraculous healing power of God in the lives of the Pylants, you may find yourself visiting that place of mystery and discovery as well. You too may sense that you are briefly touching that place of divine and perfect love—a love that awaits us all beyond the shadows of this life's short valley.

ENDNOTE

1. Kathryn Kuhlman, "Kathryn Kuhlman, Franklin, PA," The Kathryn Kuhlman Foundation, YouTube posting, accessed 7/29/2011.

INTRODUCTION

JOHNS HOPKINS HOSPITAL—BALTIMORE, MARYLAND, JANUARY 1985

When my wife Carole and I were told by the doctors that there was no hope to cure our three-year-old son, a desperate search for a miracle began. Christopher was our promised seed to carry on the family name. If he were to die, it would be devastating for us and would dash all hope for a future generation. We quickly came to realize that the only hope for his survival lay in the sovereignty of a Supreme Being.

Sadly, there are many who believe they are in control of their destiny; some actually believe there are no absolutes and that all power to succeed comes from within. This extremely destructive way of thinking has crept, in many ways, into the mainstream of our society today. The author of this most powerful and deceptive philosophy is no other than Satan, the archenemy of all humanity. There is One who has come to deliver us from this evil.

Our tenacious quest for a miracle took us on a long and faith-trying voyage, culminating in an intense ambulance race to Johns Hopkins Hospital in Baltimore, Maryland. Christopher was rushed into emergency where he lay paralyzed, comatose, and barely breathing. After being examined, he was soon placed in the caring hands of Dr. Benjamin S. Carson.

Carole and I continued facing battles between good and evil that struck crisis after crisis and spiritually challenged all who were involved.

This is a story of families of different religious traditions and natural consequences, with signs and wonders at every turn. Devastating occurrences happened in our lives that were undeserved as we fought for the life of our terminally ill child.

Our journey was one of challenged faith that was filled with surprises and is now being told to offer encouragement to all people.

Chapter 1

THE BEGINNING OF THE BATTLE

GEORGIA, LATE 1930S TO MID-1940S

Decades before my wife Carole and I battled for our son's life, the enemy viciously attacked, threatening to kill all the males that would produce heirs for future generations. I was the sixth male child born, but the only survivor of seven. In the old Pleasant Hill Baptist Church's cemetery, located in Tucker, Georgia, where many of my family members are buried, the other six boys lay silent in their graves. While they are so much a part of me, I never had a chance to know them. I have often wondered if they might be looking over the portals of heaven, cheering me on. All were either stillborn or died at a very early age. Five were my cousins; one was my brother. He was 18 months my junior and never even given a name. His grave marker simply reads: "Baby Pylant, June 23, 1944." Premature death seemed to have had a vice grip on the young male children in my father's family, almost claiming my life as well.

During my years growing up, I heard very little talk concerning their deaths. My father told me my brother wasn't carried full term and lived only two hours. Our mother's doctor diagnosed him as possibly having a defective heart. It was said that the cause of my five cousins' deaths were due to a blood defect identified as the Rh factor.

As I entered my adult years, I experienced no pressure from my parents to marry and become a father. Nevertheless, I realized it was my responsibility to produce a male child, a seed for the next generation, a legacy. Occasionally I would ask God, "Why did You allow me to live while all the other boys died?" Scripture reveals that God made man on the sixth day of His creation, and then rested, saying, "It is finished" (see Gen. 1:27-28; 2:1-2). Considering that I was the sixth male born and the only one to live, it seemed to me that God may have been saying again, "It is finished."

Unlike the story of Abraham in the Old Testament, I didn't have a messenger of the Lord appear to me, declaring I would sire a son. Nevertheless, I had faith that one day God's *promised seed* to me would be birthed.

The atmosphere of that graveyard, with its curse of death, coffins of unfulfilled promises and hopes, and chilling finality of death's seeming victory over life, would again drift into my son's hospital room years later. Prompted by the thought that there might be a curse on my family and my legacy, I refused to give in to its finality. My faith, in believing that God would not let my son die, would be stretched beyond my personal breaking point.

A FAMILY STRUGGLING TO SURVIVE

Looking back, I could easily view my childhood years through the lens of Steinbeck's *The Grapes of Wrath*, where farmers had to toil long and hard with little to no payoff.

He wrote, "In the souls of the people the grapes of wrath are filling and growing heavy, growing heavy for the vintage."[1] My parents, Aaron and Julia Pylant, were not strangers to hard work, struggling, moving, and eking out an existence. They both labored in the family's fields. Life was difficult in those days for people owning small farms, but God was always faithful to supply their needs.

My family's roots were deeply established in the Christian faith. My grandfather, George Pylant, was one of the original founders of Midway Baptist Church in Tucker, Georgia. My father served on the board of deacons there. I heard many fire and brimstone sermons preached there with the pastor warning, "This may be your last chance to receive Jesus. If you walk out that door without receiving your salvation, and die, you'll spend all of eternity in the flames of hell." Religion gave me morality and hope for eternity, but failed to fill me with the joy of an abundant life. Years later I would discover a scriptural prayer, "I pray that you prosper and be in health, even as your soul prospers" (see 3 John 2). For years, my religious mind reasoned that such a prayer would be for others but not for me or my family.

As a youth, I remember gripping the back of the pew in front of me and resisting that long walk to the front of the church to repent of my sins and receive salvation. It would be many years later, in another Baptist church, that the Holy Spirit impressed me to get out of my seat and walk the aisle to receive Jesus as my Lord and Savior.

I was very young when my father purchased the Pylant farm and old farmhouse from his family. We moved into the Tucker, Georgia, house where he had been born. Through the years, the old house had deteriorated due to neglect. It was not much of a house by today's standards. In fact, my mother told me it was more like an old southern slave shack. My parents did their best to renovate it and turn it into a home for the four of us. They wanted to give my sister Juanita and me a better life than they had growing up. While my father labored as a factory worker, my mother toiled with the job of maintaining the house and taking care of us. She became pregnant with my brother just about the time we moved there. Perhaps the hard work and the stress contributed to his early death.

The house had no electricity, no plumbing, and consequently no inside bathroom facilities. We drew water from a well located adjacent to the bottom porch steps that led to the kitchen. My mother worked very hard. Although many of our relatives and friends had the modern conveniences in their homes, I never questioned the fact that we didn't. I still smile with amusement when recalling a visit by one of my cousins who was accustomed to having those simple luxuries. As she entered the darkened house she asked, "Where's the light switch?" She was absolutely surprised when my father struck a match and lit an oil-burning lamp to illuminate the room. But the biggest shock came when she asked where the bathroom was located.

By all appearances, poverty had a stronghold on our family. Each time my parents made a little headway, something unforeseen happened that hindered their plans. They had a desire to build a new house of their own, and it was slowly becoming a reality. The house plans had been selected and the building site agreed upon. The new house was to be erected just a few feet in front of the old one. It would be nestled among a grove of beautiful oak trees that had provided shade during the hot summer months for many previous generations. The timber used to build the house was being harvested from the trees that grew on our property.

On the day the foundation was to be put in, my parents went to check on the progress being made at the sawmill. On their return they were horrified to find flames shooting out of the old house. That afternoon, my sister and I exited the school bus and walked down the long, dusty dirt road that led to our home. We were not prepared for such a horrific sight. All that remained of the old house were ashes and smoldering timbers. Our mother, father, and a few neighbors stood around a couple pieces of furniture that had been salvaged before the structure collapsed. Earlier that day we were just another poor family. Now we were both poor *and* homeless!

Surveying my past, poverty, destruction, and death seemed to cloak our family with a chilling fog that drifted insidiously into our lives every time we tried to find our way into the American dream and the hope that God's plans for us were good and not evil. For a moment, things began to look up. Many good and generous people rallied around us. They supplied food, clothing, and shelter. Uncle Paul and Aunt Dolly graciously invited us to share their home while our new house was being built.

As the old adage goes, when you hit rock bottom the only way to go is up. Being a positive man, *that* was exactly the direction in which my father was determined to go. With much hard work, prayer, and trusting the Lord for guidance, he was finally able to move his family into our new home, providing us a new way of life. Now, we too had the long-awaited "modern" conveniences!

I am eternally grateful to have witnessed my parents' faith in God and their bullish tenacity to overcome poverty. It gave me an inherited deep-seated, powerful kind of confidence that would strengthen me to face the devastating obstacles that later threatened to bury my faith.

Endnote

1.   John Steinbeck, *Grapes of Wrath* (New York: Penguin Books, orig. 1939), 349.

Chapter 2

GAINS AND LOSSES

GEORGIA, 1969

I said "I do" in marriage when I was 23; and three years later my wife gave birth to our beautiful daughter, Heather Elaine. In those days, there was no way to determine the sex of the unborn child. We had painted the nursery blue in anticipation of a boy. We put blue carpet on the floor and hung blue and white curtains at the windows. However, as silly as it sounds, while shopping for nursery furniture, we both fell in love with a white canopy bed. Maybe something inside of us was saying, "You *are* having a girl." Purchasing the bed was a smart move. It not only complemented the room, but it fit Heather perfectly. It was beautiful and dainty, just like her.

Heather's birth was a partial fulfillment of God's promised seed to me. I knew that He wanted me to be "fruitful and multiply" in every area of life (see Gen. 1:28), including having children. My wonderful daughter was the first fruit of my coming children—at least, that was my hope. But hope was short-lived—another loss was around the corner.

Heather became the light of my life. I couldn't wait to come home after work to spend every evening with her. My wife and I both enjoyed so much watching Heather grow. She was a smart, quick-to-learn little girl. One of the most joyful times I remember with her was at bedtime. From bath time to bedtime, my little angel could make my heart smile. Every night we sang songs, and every night she begged, "Just one more song, Daddy, please." We had a good routine going on!

Sadly, the happy times we shared as a family came to an end, as did our marriage. We were divorced in May 1972, when Heather was only three years old. Her mother remarried shortly afterward. My visitation with my daughter became more strained and difficult. I quickly came to believe that the feelings of a father are often ignored. I suddenly found myself as only a part-time parent. My home and family life had always been a high priority for me. But when the bottom fell out, instead of turning to God for comfort and guidance, I started to party almost every night in an attempt to ease the pain and to fill the void in my life.

I had lost a spouse and continual contact with my daughter. My hope for a promised seed to carry on the family name seemed so remote. Emptiness, loneliness, and abandonment seemed like my destiny. Looking for love in all the wrong places, my life was adrift and my hope was reduced to a fragile flicker of light.

A RAY OF HOPE—GEORGIA, 1972

In May 1972, Carole Zinz moved from Maryland to Atlanta, Georgia, to fill the position of buyer and coordinator for lady's sportswear in the same store in which I worked.

We were introduced in August of 1972. I asked her on a date and she refused; but I persisted and she finally gave in. We had our first date in October and steadily spent more and more time together.

Later, she tried to ease my mind when she told me, "The reason I didn't want to go out with you wasn't because you weren't good looking or charming. It was because I didn't want to get involved with a man who was divorced and already had a child."

In December of that same year, Carole invited me to travel with her to Baltimore, Maryland. Her parents, Frances and Oscar Zinz, were celebrating their 35th wedding anniversary. Our families were of different faiths. Her father was raised in the Orthodox Jewish synagogue and was a direct descendant of the Levite tribe. Her mother was taught in the Reformed Jewish temple and was from the tribe of Dan. Being raised in the Baptist church, and from the "tribe of Jesus," made me wonder if they would have a problem if their daughter seriously dated a Christian. But my concerns were soon put to rest when I discovered that Carole and her two sisters, Terry and Sandy, had been raised in the Reformed temple, which was more open to interfaith relationships.

When we arrived at the anniversary party, I was glad to find none of the guys were wearing yarmulkes or prayer shawls. Thankfully, no one was speaking Hebrew or Yiddish. If they had, I would have surely stood out from the crowd, speaking with a southern drawl and dressed in a two-piece "faux-suede" suit.

The buffet seemed a bit strange to my palate. I had never eaten a bagel with lox, liver pate, or pickled herring. Needless to say, none of my usual diet was on the menu. I could not find any ham, black-eyed peas, collard greens, or cornbread anywhere on the table but I still enjoyed a sampling of everything. Having a sweet tooth, I especially loved the delicious desserts like rainbow cake and baklava.

Carole's parents were very gracious and all of their friends and family members were very warm and friendly. While there, Carole, Terry, and Sandy showed me the sights of Baltimore.

Two months later in February 1973, we were engaged. We were honored to receive blessings from Carole's parents. We, but especially I, held our breath anticipating how her family's Rabbi, Rabbi Shusterman, would counsel us. With a sigh of relief, we were happy to have received his blessings also. I felt the most anxious about all of this because it went way beyond just having that chat with her father. This seemed over the top to me, but I did it *and I survived!*

Carole wanted to be married in her parent's home; so on May 19, 1973, her dream came true. My mother-in-law, Frances, prepared a beautiful setting for our wedding. We exchanged our vows under a canopy erected in the living room with Rabbi Shusterman officiating.

Carole was a beautiful and radiant bride as she strolled down the long hallway on her father's arm. My father stood with me as my best man. One of the highlights of the ceremony was my daughter Heather, who served as our beautiful and precious flower girl.

After the wedding ceremony, Carole and I proceeded to the receiving line. The Zinz's home was large enough to accommodate the more than 60 guests who attended. As we greeted the guests, the room was transformed into a party atmosphere with live music. After the four-tier wedding cake was cut and served, the party officially began. My mother-in-law later told Carole and me that many of the guests commented on how they enjoyed the intimacy of our home wedding. We had definitely accomplished our goal!

As I would later learn, great significance was imparted to our future seed (descendants) and generations with this union of a Jewish woman and a Christian man. At this point in my life, I did not have a close relationship with God, nor did I understand how the God of Abraham, Isaac, and Jacob would bring an "Isaac" into our lives—a son who would truly bless not only us and our families, but also future generations. Nor could I imagine once having a child, a namesake for our family, we would be faced with the mysterious and horrific choice of putting him on an altar of sacrifice, giving him up, even as Abraham, the father of the Jews, had done with his son Isaac thousands of years before.

I share this as context and a backdrop to what seemed to be a simple, interfaith marriage, but was in fact the beginning of a journey of faith that would be tested at every turn. Yes, a ray of hope had dispelled the ever-present shadows in my life. But such hope proved fleeting and storms were already rising on the horizon.

After our wedding, we settled into our new home in Decatur, Georgia, which I had purchased before we were married. We became a family and Carole loved my daughter as if she were her own child. When Heather came to visit us, Carole always went out of her way to shower her with love, assuring her that our home was her home as well. What a joy it was to be in a happy marriage with my only child living nearby. However, this honeymoon world would eventually cease and life's tests would soon disrupt our marriage.

ANOTHER LOSS, BUT WAIT... —BALTIMORE, MARYLAND, 1975

We had lived in our Decatur home only two years when Carole's father, Oscar, approached us about moving to Baltimore. He wanted us to work with him in the family-owned furniture business. Carole said she would leave that decision entirely up to me.

There seemed to be so much to consider. It would mean not only leaving Heather behind, but also abandoning the work in cosmetology that I had recently started. But we did have an out. Carole and I agreed that if things didn't work out, we would move back to Georgia. After six months of consideration, we sold our home in September 1975, and bid a very difficult and heartfelt good-bye to Heather and my family.

It was like losing my daughter all over again. No longer would we live close and be able to see one another often. While I knew the decision to move seemed to be a good financial decision for us, I did not know what the future held for our family. My heart ached to have a son, but we needed the financial stability to expand our family. So I tried to create a future for us that would make it possible for God to fulfill His promises. Instead of trusting Him as our source, we thought that our plans, hard work, and efforts would improve our future as a family. We would soon learn that God had other plans for our journey.

During the first year, while working with the furniture store, Carole and I saw the writing on the wall. The company was having severe financial problems. Baltimore had gone through a tremendous growth period. Suburban stores had pulled a lot of trade from the downtown area. The Harbor area was also booming, having a negative effect on the retail establishments that remained in the older part of the city.

My father-in-law's business eventually folded. It was understandable that Carole was reluctant to move back to Georgia at that time, leaving her family in turmoil, having to close the doors to their business that had sustained them for more than two generations. Suddenly, we found ourselves among the unemployed.

Yet another loss would blight our future. I could still return to doing what I had done in the past—cosmetology. I have a friend who says that when you have lost your harvest, go back to sowing what's in your hand. I hadn't lost my skill or potential; so, once again, I would move from the night of loss to the flickering sunlight of hope for a brighter future. I believed that God was guiding even when I couldn't see what the future held. He simply gave enough light for one step at a time. So I took the next step.

I quickly located a salon in which I leased a workstation to pursue my craft in the world of cosmetology. It was located in a good area, on the first floor of the Charles Building across the street from Johns Hopkins University. At the time, unisex hair cutting was in its infancy. By advertising and targeting the students and faculty at the university, I began to build a good clientele base.

After deciding not to move back to Georgia, we felt it was time to purchase a home. We believed this move to be a good investment for our future. We had the equity from the sale of our home in Decatur for a down payment. Unfortunately, the houses in the area we preferred to live were too expensive, forcing us to consider other options. Our search took us farther north, to York, Pennsylvania, where we purchased a house of ample size and in our price range. Its location was in close proximity to Interstate 695, offering an easy, one-hour commute to my work. Carole took employment as buyer with a local family-owned store specializing in ladies apparel.

My plan was to also seek employment in York. Before that could happen, however, a hair salon became available for purchase near the shop where I worked. We bought the business (with owner financing) in September 1978. And my commute continued for the next six years.

Carole and I loved our new home but soon realized there was something missing. We longed to hear the sound of a child's laughter. Carole had never been married. Like most young brides, she looked forward to becoming a mom. During our engagement, we discussed the possibility of having children. Since there was a difference in our religious beliefs, a choice would have to be made about which faith they would be taught. We both agreed on the Christian faith. We also agreed, if we had a boy, his name would be Christopher O'Neal.

We were not getting any younger—I had celebrated 37 years and Carole was younger, at 35. I knew Carole would be a loving mother. However, I had a more difficult time making a commitment to having a child because of the conflict and heartache I endured with the breakup of my first marriage. I allowed a fear of possibly being separated from another child to almost consume me. But this wasn't about me; it was about God's plan for a future, a legacy, and blessings to be poured out on others even when I couldn't imagine what the future might hold. Without realizing it, a seed of faith in me would triumph over a harvest of fear, doubt, and loss that I had reaped for years. I would stand amazed that so little faith could result in such great blessing.

Again, although I had not asked Him for His guidance, God, in His infinite wisdom, looked out for me. Please understand this: God is faithful even when we are not (see 2 Tim. 2:13). I would learn this lesson over and over again. My efforts had not secured our future; but God had our future in His hands and by grace, not hard work, we would experience unspeakable joy for a moment.

THE PROMISED CHILD— TOWSON, MARYLAND, 1981

In the spring of 1980, Carole's doctor confirmed that we were going to be parents. By that time our little hair salon was doing well financially, giving Carole the option to stop work during her pregnancy. How exciting this was for us. The shadows of that cemetery graveyard were melting away in the light of this news that we would have a child. Still, as it had been with my firstborn, modern technology had not perfected the science to tell us what the sex of the baby would be. My hope, thoughts, and prayers were that we would have a son to carry on my family's name. Of course, first of all, my concern was for Carole and the baby's health and safety. We were in our 30s, so we knew that this would probably be the one and only child we would have together. We would rejoice and be wonderfully blessed with a boy or a girl.

Carole's obstetrician, Dr. Kelly, was located in Towson, Maryland, about an hour-drive from our home. Her delivery date was to be sometime after mid-January. The weather can turn nasty in Pennsylvania and Maryland during the winter, so our plan was to go to Carole's sister's house when her contraction pains were still safely spaced. We were there only one night when, in the wee hours of the morning, Carole's water broke. We rushed her to the Greater Baltimore Medical Center located in Towson. While we prayed continually for a safe and quick delivery, her labor lasted all day and stretched into the night.

This baby did not make delivery easy due the size of his head. We had attended childbirth classes during Carole's pregnancy, feeling we were prepared for anything. However, believe me, when a soon-to-be father has gone into the birthing room and tries to comfort his wife, she is not always receptive to his interpretation of how or when to breathe. It's interesting that our son's birth happened at night. So much of our journey has been a battle against the darkness. For us, light conquered the darkness and our joy overflowed!

Our son, Christopher O'Neal Pylant, was born January 23, 1981, at 9:05 p.m. His birth marked the eighth year of our marriage. The biblical number *eight* is for new beginnings. What a thrill it was to hear Dr. Kelly announce, "It's a boy!" A nurse cleaned our newborn child, wrapped him in a blanket, and then gently placed him in my arms. I looked into the face of my promised seed for the first time and spoke softly, "Hello, Christopher!" He was so alert and responsive to all the sounds. He tried to open his little eyes when I spoke. He jerked when a bell rang in the delivery room.

The nurse then took Christopher from me and placed him in his mother's arms. With tears of joy in her eyes, she kissed her son's face and said, "I love you, Christopher." Observing this tender and loving scene, mother with child, and being in total awe of God's beautiful creation, the fear I once had of losing another child through a possible divorce vanished. God had been faithful in blessing me with my promised seed. Now Christopher could carry on the family name.

Carole bonded to her newborn son immediately. During her pregnancy, she had talked to her child in the womb, prayed, sang soothing songs, and tried to take good care of her health. She felt honored that God would allow her to be part of this life-giving process. She prayed, "Lord, if I only am able to have one child, please let this child be a boy." Now it was confirmed, God had heard her prayers and brought her the son she had longed for.

As far as pregnancies go, nothing was unusual, but she did have one really bad scare in her last trimester. While going down the steps into the basement one day while home alone, she slipped on a step and began to fall. She tried to balance herself between the wall and the railing, but missed a few steps and landed on her bottom with a jolt. She immediately prayed, "Please God, let this baby be okay and let no harm come to it." Already realizing that this baby was a gift from God, she felt His love flowing through the child inside of her. Sometimes we learn about love in very special ways.

A deep passion and desire arose in her to be the best mother and to make God proud of her. Fear gripped her as she thought about how she could have injured our baby when she fell, but faith was stronger and we both realized that the Lord had the situation under control. Delivery was difficult and extremely uncomfortable, but all the pain of childbirth was soon forgotten as God's promised seed brought glorious light into our lives the night of Christopher's birth. With unspeakable joy, Carole and I stepped into a bright and hopeful future with our new son.

Babies Are Awesome Gifts— York, Pennsylvania, 1981

Now that we were home with our little bundle of joy, our marriage and our lives were more complete. Though Carole and I had agreed to raise Christopher in the Christian faith, she asked if I would honor her and her family by allowing him to have a Bris Milah: a Jewish ceremony in which the male child is circumcised on the eighth day after his birth. To the Jewish people, this ceremony is a celebration of a new life, a new beginning. This seemed logical because Christopher was born during the eighth year of our marriage and eight stood for new beginnings, giving new life for the next Pylant generation.

Christopher was circumcised in the Jewish tradition. He was placed on a table while all the family stood to observe. The Mohel, who performed the circumcision, placed a wine soaked piece of surgical gauze in Christopher's mouth to minimize the pain. Then he placed a sharp surgical instrument at the tip of his penis and quickly removed the foreskin.

During a Bris Milah ceremony, it is customary for the child to receive a Hebrew name. We chose Emanuel, Carole's father's middle name. On that day, January 31, 1981, our son was named Christopher O'Neal Emanuel Pylant. How special and meaningful were the names given to him! *Christopher* means "bearer or follower of Christ," *Neal* means "champion," and *Emanuel* means "God with us."

Our blond-haired, blue-eyed little package of energy grew and reached all normal benchmarks of development. Christopher's checkups with his pediatrician found him to be a healthy and happy little boy. He filled our home and our hearts with much joy and happiness. He loved books and singing at a very early age.

Since I was taking voice lessons at that time, Christopher and I enjoyed practicing our music together. "New York, New York" was his favorite song. He belted out its lyrics into the microphone of our karaoke machine.

In many wonderful ways, I felt there was something different in Christopher, something unusually special. Maybe, like every other proud father, I was simply being prejudiced. But then, to our surprise, we began to hear from other people, especially strangers, what they noticed about him. Once at an open-air shopping center, a lady saw him from a distance. She hurried to catch up with us, saying, "I just had to see your little boy up close. I could almost swear I saw an aura of light around him. There is something so special about him!" Those words were not exactly the normal "run of the mill" comment anyone would say about a child. I thought it was a little strange at the time but tried not to analyze it too much. Much later, we would recall this encounter and wonder if what this lady had seen was the radiant presence of angels surrounding Christopher.

Not having both families near to enjoy the special events in Christopher's life, we traveled back to Georgia as often as possible to visit my family. I have treasured memories of my father enjoying the special times with his long-awaited grandson. They fed the birds in the backyard, fished in my dad's beautiful, ten-acre lake, and often groomed Charley, the family's beloved white, longhair tomcat. For two years my father enjoyed his grandson. While I rejoice in those two years, I still felt robbed of even more because, once again, a shadowy fog descended upon our family.

Chapter 3

THROUGH THE VALLEY OF
THE SHADOW OF DEATH

YORK, PENNSYLVANIA, JANUARY 1983

A few weeks had passed after spending the Christmas holiday with my family in December 1982. I received a telephone call from Juanita, my sister, informing me that our father had been taken to the hospital. He was suffering severe chest pains. His doctor was keeping him under observation and shared concern that a heart attack might occur. I spoke with my father by phone that evening. He said he felt a lot better as he watched his favorite television program.

The next day, January 23, 1983, a few friends along with Carole's family gathered for a little party to celebrate Christopher's second birthday. He had already blown out the little candles adorning his birthday cake and was patiently waiting to open his colorfully wrapped presents. The telephone rang. I rushed to answer it thinking it might be someone calling to wish Christopher a happy birthday. Instead, I heard the frantic voice of my sister telling me our father had suffered a severe heart attack. The doctor advised me to come as soon as possible because if he had another attack within a certain period of time, it could be fatal.

Plans were made for the first flight out of Baltimore/ Washington International Airport. Ironically, my flight was scheduled at 9:05 p.m., the exact time of Christopher's birth. My sister-in-law Terry and a friend, Gerri Aronin, drove me to the airport. The flight was delayed because of a snow and ice storm in the northern state from which the plane was traveling. After about an hour wait, I said good-bye to Terry and Gerri and then boarded the plane.

Settled into the flight, I reached up, turned off the overhead light, and gazed out the window. I felt the damp, dark fog drifting in, the same darkness I had felt in the graveyard. My thoughts drifted back to the day when we were about to leave for the Atlanta airport after spending the Christmas holiday with my family. I remembered walking into the living room and noticing a little Christian booklet laying on a table beside my father's favorite chair. It had been given to me about 15 years earlier. I was surprised to find that it had mysteriously reappeared. When asking my father about the booklet, he insisted I take it home with me and read a particular passage from the Bible found in John 14:1-4:

> *Do not let your hearts be troubled. You believe in God; believe also in Me. My Father's house has many rooms; if that were not so, would I have told you that I am going there to prepare a place for you? And if I go and prepare a place for you, I will come back and*

take you to be with Me that you also may be where I am. You know the way to the place where I am going (NIV).

I had heard these verses before during church services, but I didn't realize that when my father asked me to read them, just how meaningful they would become. They proved to be welcomed comfort in my time of sadness and grief.

"Sir, excuse me. Sir. Would you care for something?" I had drifted so deeply into thought that I hadn't noticed the flight attendant serving refreshments.

"Yes, thank you. Coffee, with cream please," I replied.

With coffee in hand, I returned my gaze out the window to observe the awesome beauty of the universe. The moon was shining brightly against the billowing white clouds. The stars were twinkling with brilliance against the dark night sky—there were so many that my mind couldn't possibly conceive their numbers. I'd once heard a preacher say that God calls each star by its name. Suddenly, a strange unexplainable feeling came over me. I could only think that the Lord had already called my father by his name and his spirit had departed from his body and traveled to its final destination. While I felt a grief that was sadly selfish, I could smile knowing that he was in the arms of his heavenly Father.

My daughter Heather and a cousin met me at the Atlanta airport. It was not a surprise to learn my father had already died. Hearing of his passing gave me a deeper spiritual connection to God and confirmation that the experience I had during the flight was of the Holy Spirit. I believe the Scripture

found in John—the one that my father asked me to read—
was a message given to me also, a message that set the stage
for his impending death. Many times, when God speaks to
us or shows us something, we often hear it in muffled tones
or see the vision as if looking through shattered eyeglasses.
Then, when the foretold message unfolds, we can hear with
perfect sound and see with 20/20 vision.

My father's death certificate records his time of death to
be 9:10 p.m. Nevertheless, there's reason to believe he died
in my mother's arms before she was ushered from the room.
During the few minutes that followed, my daughter watched
through a glass door with its blinds only partially closed
as the doctor unsuccessfully attempted to revive her Papa.
Many things that occurred later made me believe my father's
time of death was indeed 9:05 p.m., the exact time as my
scheduled flight from Baltimore. I couldn't help but make
the symbolic connection that it was the exact time of Christopher's birth just two years earlier. The promised seed had
brought light into our lives. Christopher's grandfather, now
a star of righteousness, had departed this world. His generational seed, connected by the light through three generations,
was deposited now in Christopher.

Unknown to any of us at the time, the war between light
and darkness was about to explode onto the battleground of
our lives.

TRANSITIONS—YORK,
PENNSYLVANIA, JANUARY 1983

I find it interesting that God uses transitions to position us
for the next season in our life. The question isn't, "God, why

are You doing this?" The question is, "Will I be obedient to follow Your plan?"

After my father's passing, Carole had a jolting experience. One day as she was looking out the window, a vision of my father appeared to her. With compassionate eyes and a warm smile, it seemed as if he was there to comfort her. She sensed that he was saying, "Don't worry, Carole, everything will be all right." She was puzzled, because, at that time, everything seemed to be fine. Sometime later, however, an unsettling feeling that "something" was going to happen to Christopher in two years began to trouble her.

Not long after having the vision of my father, Carole had an unexplainable desire to move back to Georgia. Her feeling of urgency became so intense that we eventually sold our hair salon. I continued to work, leasing a workstation, until we sold our home. Carole's family was very concerned that we were moving and there really was no rational way to explain this to them. In fact, we didn't really understand it ourselves. It was as if, without realizing it, a spiritual force was directing our path. I often relate our experience to Abram's. God told him, "Leave your country and family and go" (see Gen. 12:1-4). However, unlike Abram's command, we were at least told where to go but the *why* was yet to be revealed.

It was Labor Day weekend, 1984, when we began our long drive to Georgia. Our furniture and most of our belongings were already in route south via Mayflower Moving Vans. A small U-Haul trailer was hitched to Carole's Chevrolet Camero and contained some of the more personal and sentimental things. Christopher, strapped securely in his car seat, traveled very happily with his mother, and I followed in my own car. During our almost 11 years of marriage, Carole and I had already moved five times. We were beginning to feel like nomads on the move again. The difference was that this time we were traveling to a destination without clearly understanding the purpose.

We were totally exhausted by the time we arrived at our new place, a leased three-bedroom, two-bath apartment located in Lilburn, Georgia. Being that we had traveled such a long distance while pulling a U-Haul, and being especially concerned for the comfort and safety of our little one, this trip could not be considered a joy ride.

We had moved with no promise of employment and had to rely on the equity from the sale of our home and hair salon to sustain us until we were otherwise financially re-established.

Fortunately, I soon secured a job with a salon near our home. My plan was to work for a while to build a personal client base, and then perhaps buy my own salon again. Carole quickly enrolled Christopher in a school program. At three years and seven months old, he seemed to enjoy his new environment and looked forward each day to meeting with his playmates at school.

My mother and sister were happy that we had made a decision to move back home to Georgia. Heather, now almost 16, seemed elated to have her little brother and the entire family close again. In many ways we had been deprived of being close during her years growing up. Living so far apart, we were not able to be there personally to share the special times in her life, putting more strain on our father-daughter relationship. Now that we were home in Georgia, we began to mend the hurts that many times occur when a family is torn apart by divorce.

How important family is. My children, my biological family, and now my in-laws were all connected with Judeo-Christian roots—faith in the living God of Abraham, Isaac, and Jacob—and ready for the future. At least, I thought we were ready by being in the best of all worlds and relationships, but all that would be tested. Paul wrote, *"Tribulation worketh patience"* (Rom. 5:3 KJV); that is to say endurance, patience, and tenacity. The shadows were lengthening and the storm clouds were gathering.

THE WORLD BEGAN TO SPIN—LILBURN, GEORGIA, SEPTEMBER 1984

Heather was dating a young man named Raymond. He played quarterback with their high school football team. She invited us to bring Christopher to watch Raymond play. The next day our three-year-old Christopher was still excited about the game. He said to me, "Dad, let's play football. You tackle me."

I rolled him onto the floor and walked away. When I heard him moaning, I looked around and asked, "What's wrong with you?"

He said, "I'm dizzy. I can't get up!" I immediately rushed over and picked him up to make sure he was all right. We had noticed him tilting his head to the right a few days earlier. The dizziness prompted us to consult Dr. Matthews, his pediatrician. Christopher was treated with medication due to an ear infection. A week later, Carole took him back to the doctor's office for a follow-up examination. The ear infection had cleared, while the tilting of his head continued. Carole asked Dr. Matthews about the tilting of his head and was assured that it had become a habit because of the ear problem. The doctor said it would correct itself soon, not to worry.

It was a bright cheerful day in October, somewhat warm for the season but still comfortable enough to endure without air conditioning. Christopher was busy playing in the family room, trying his best to prolong the inevitable naptime. He was home from school that day. It was nearing the time to put him down for his usual afternoon nap. If given a choice between taking an afternoon nap, watching Bert and Ernie, or pretending to be young David from the Bible who slew the great, big, bad Goliath, honestly, an afternoon nap would definitely be his third choice. I called to Christopher and reminded him of the time. Soon, I heard him making his way to the hall bathroom. The sound of a flushing toilet and the splashing water from the sink told me that he had been obedient to have gone potty and wash his hands. Before retiring to his bed, I opened a window so we could enjoy the freshness of an autumn breeze. I had already selected two books containing some of his favorite stories.

We were laughing and talking as I read to him. Touching the back of his neck, I discovered it was covered with perspiration. I said, "Let's take off your t-shirt so you will be cooler."

As I lifted the shirt over his head, he began to cry out, "Daddy, Daddy, there's something wrong with me." I picked him up and stood him on the floor, but he could not stand on his own. I held him with my arms around his waist as he went limp and began to vomit. We were home alone, as

Carole had gone out to grocery shop. Still vomiting, I carried him to the bathroom and placed cool, wet washcloths on his face.

When his vomiting subsided, I dashed to the telephone and placed an anxious call to Dr. Matthews's office. Carole returned from the store while I was on the telephone. We were advised to take Christopher to an eye, ear, nose, and throat specialist. Dr. Matthews's nurse gave us the telephone number of the specialist's office. Having a referral from Christopher's pediatrician and the urgency at hand, we were able to see the specialist that afternoon. Carole quickly put fresh clothing on Christopher and wrapped him in a blanket while I put away her purchases from the store. Without delay, we rushed Christopher to the doctor's office.

The results of the examination puzzled all of us. There was no sign of an inner ear infection. The specialist said, "I don't know what is wrong with your son, but I can tell you that *he is a very sick little boy.*" We left there and went immediately to the pediatrician's office. A series of blood tests began. With no conclusive results from the blood tests, Dr. Matthews had difficulty pinpointing the cause of Christopher's illness. Unable to give a diagnosis, Dr. Matthews advised us to see a neurologist, Dr. Herbert Schub, for his opinion. Carole and I prayed that he would be able to give us concrete answers to our son's illness and put us on the road to his recovery.

THE GATHERING STORMS

We told Dr. Schub about all the symptoms we had noticed and all that had been done to determine the cause of Christopher's illness. With Dr. Matthews having no conclusive results from the blood tests and no further testing done, he too was unable to come to any rational conclusions or diagnoses. Because of Christopher's young age, he preferred not to X-ray his head but urged us to closely monitor him and report any changes in his condition. If Dr. Schub suspected a neurological problem at that time, he didn't share it with us.

Feelings of frustration, fear, anxiety, and, yes, even anger, were pushing us further into a fog of confusion that would persist for months. The cause for Christopher's illness and a diagnosis could not be given; it was infuriating! We both wondered, *With all the medical technology and testing available, what was taking so long? How could these educated men not recognize exactly what was going on and then fix it?*

Dr. Matthews could only render an educated guess. It was the best he could do, but for us it was just not enough. He finally concluded that a germ *might have* remained in Christopher's body from a previous illness, causing a deterioration of his immune system. Precautionary measures were taken. Christopher was immediately quarantined. At that time, we had seen on television and read in magazine articles of a little boy whose immune system had been weakened so severely that it became necessary for him to live in a bubble. If Dr. Matthews's conclusion was correct, and Christopher didn't respond to treatment, our greatest fear would be that he might have to be isolated from others.

Carole and Christopher remained quarantined in the apartment. When coming home from work, I showered and changed clothes before having any contact with him for fear of transferring a germ. For Christopher, it was like being held prisoner against his own free will. His only escape from the house was to make weekly visits to the doctor's office for a set of four very painful injections. The injections were for hemoglobin to rebuild his red blood cell count. They would boost his energy level for a few days but then the signs of weakness would return. The quarantine stretched to two long, agonizing months.

When his left eye began to cross slightly, we thought perhaps he had been watching too much television and thus causing excessive eyestrain. Then we noticed he was becoming more lethargic. The hemoglobin injections seemed to have less and less effect on his energy level. He began to stagger when he walked. Many times he was greeted in the morning hours with the dry heaves. Palsy gradually crept over the left side of his face and his physical condition quickly deteriorated.

We were watching a ravaging sickness engulf him day by day and our hearts were breaking. We felt helpless. It was like the stories of those hiding in an inner closet or bathroom waiting for the approaching storm or tornado. You don't know when it will hit or what will happen, but you know that disaster is approaching and you can't do anything about it. So we huddled at home, waiting for the storm to pass and an all-clear siren to sound, but that didn't happen.

No Light at the End of the Tunnel— Atlanta, Georgia, November 1984

Observing the rapid decline in Christopher's condition, Dr. Matthews advised us to see Dr. Schub for a second examination. At this point, he obviously knew that it had to be more than just an immune deficiency. In my heart, I am sure that he suspected a neurological problem. He did not want to alarm us and render a diagnosis without the neurological test results in his hand to back him up. But still I think he knew. It's like a meteorologist seeing all the radar tracking and watching the conditions arise for a perfect storm, but not wanting to alarm the public until necessary.

Dr. Schub put Christopher through a series of neurological tests: eye coordination, muscle reflexes, tongue rotation, and walking and running exercises. After the examination, we all waited intensely for the results as many memories of earlier occurrences flooded my mind. It's mysterious how little things in life can be overlooked until there is a crisis. Even though Carole had a near perfect pregnancy, there had been a problem with delivery because of Christopher's head size. His head measurement was very close to the abnormal range, but her obstetrician said there was no cause for alarm. Could there have been any connection between that observation and what was now happening?

As Christopher grew, he had good eye-hand coordination, but his gross motor skills were never up to par. As a baby, he crawled backward. When he could run, he often leaned slightly to the right. Many times I commented to Carole that Christopher's head seemed to be abnormally large.

We concluded it might have been a genetic inheritance from generations past. I recalled these observations and now wondered if they were signals that we didn't recognize and deal with. Were we to blame because we saw these things and just didn't do anything about them? Hindsight often causes us to blame ourselves or even condemn others. However, such reactions often distract us from the issue at hand and finding the right path through the storm. We could not be distracted. We had to fight through our emotions, doubts, and regrets.

There were so many different thoughts and emotions that surged through us, but the biggest issue remained ahead of us. No one could tell us what was wrong with him, and, without a diagnosis, no healing possibilities existed. We found ouselves in a dark tunnel moving forward but no light ahead. We couldn't go back and we feared going forward. We wanted answers, and we wanted them yesterday.

I took Christopher to the restroom. In my thoughts, I could not wrap my mind around the idea that this beautiful child, the light of my life, could have anything wrong with him—let alone something serious or major. Carole sat alone in that room and waited. Neither of us were prepared for the report that would soon shake our world.

Chapter 4

NOT HELPLESS OR HOPELESS

ATLANTA, GEORGIA, NOVEMBER 1984

Before I returned with Christopher, the doctor walked into the room and announced his verdict, "Mrs. Pylant, I believe Christopher has a brain tumor." Those matter-of-fact words hit her like a sledgehammer!

"A brain tumor? Exactly, what does that mean?" Carole knew deep inside the crevices of her soul that this was not good news. She began to shake uncontrollably as she thought, *Will I lose my son? No! This could not be happening to us. No way is this real!*

In a quick flashback, Carole remembered losing her father-in-law, dying on Christopher's second birthday. That recall now cast an ominous feeling of the "what-ifs" in her mind. Would she see darkness now overshadowing Christopher's life? She sat there in utter shock. Her heart pounded. Tears flooded her countenance as she grilled herself, "What have I done wrong? Is this my fault? God, can You hear me? I desperately need Your help."

I returned to the room with Christopher at that moment, seeing my wife completely overwhelmed with emotions. I whispered, "What's wrong?"

"Dr. Scrub will explain," Carole sobbed.

She took our son into her arms and held him so close as if her embrace could protect him from the dark monster that lurked in the shadows. We were headed for uncharted territories—places where none of us had ever been or even wanted to visit.

As Carole tightly held Christopher, I knew something was not right as I watched her interact with him. Dr. Schub took me aside and reported to me his suspicions of a brain tumor as well. I felt like I had been punched in the gut—the kind where your breath is knocked out of you and you struggle to take in the next one. I wanted to reach into my child's body and rip out every bit of that tumor in Christopher's brain.

Of course, I couldn't do that, but I wanted to do something. However, for that moment in time, there was nothing I could do—I felt so helpless and hopeless. I had to get myself together and be supportive for Carole. I felt that I could not show worry or fear to my son. All my acting abilities came to life in that instant! I had to put on the performance of my life—at least for the time.

Our son was immediately admitted to Scottish Rite Children's Hospital; and for a brain scan to be taken, he was transferred to Northside Hospital, which was located across the street.

This is totally unbelievable, I thought as I watched our sedated son lying motionless on the table as the scan began. If someone would have asked me to tell them what feelings I had at that moment, I could not give just one or two words. Every feeling known to humankind was swirling in my mind. The love for my child catapulted me into survival mode. "He must live. After all, he is just a child." I know that I personally felt threatened. God's promised seed faced possible extinction from our family line. I needed to do something—anything— to save my son. I was his daddy; yet I couldn't fix this or make it go away. Waves of rage and powerlessness sent shock waves through me. I can remember thinking, *Surely, I'll wake up from this and find it all has been just a horrible nightmare.* Unfortunately, it was not just an emotional darkness or a horrible nightmare. We were standing face to face with a harsh reality that was straight from hell—impending death.

No one felt it more than Carole. While Christopher and I were in for the scan, she paced the halls in total shock and disbelief. What does a mother's love look like when her child's life is being threatened? Overwhelmed with all emotions, Carole felt totally alone. She was waiting outside the scan room in a long, open hallway lined with windows whose light could not overcome her dark thoughts. However, the warm sunlight helped her feel that God was close and revealing Himself to her through those warm rays. They almost seemed to thaw those stiff, frozen veins of fear that had wrapped around her heart.

Carole talked to God and kept pacing the floor, asking what she had done wrong and what she needed to do to make things right. She wanted to believe that the results would prove that the position of the tumor would make it possible and easy for the surgeons to remove this unwanted leech that was sucking the life out of our son. Still, the clouds of a bad report kept bringing her back to the worst-case scenario—a malignant, non-operable tumor that was so deeply embedded and entwined around his spinal cord that surgery was not even an option.

She wanted answers. Why had this happened? What would the future hold for Christopher? He was so full of life. He loved to read books, listen to music, sing, feed the ducks at the park, and he loved his preschool classes. What did all this mean for him?

How in the world would she ever tell her parents that their grandson was facing a life and death situation? Carole got the phone to call her parents, but felt paralyzed. She would pick up the phone and then put it down with a thump, wrestling with how long she could keep them in the dark. She desperately wanted to have some ray of light to share with them but felt flooded with darkness.

The reality struck her full force again. She really was in the hospital waiting for more testing to end. Minutes seemed like hours. She longed to hold Christopher again in her arms. What was taking so long?

With legs that felt like concrete blocks, Carole wobbled her way to the phone down the hall and called her parents. Her mother answered the phone. She tried to hold back the tears and to be brave. She asked, "Is Dad there?"

"No, Carole, what's wrong? You are scaring me," her mother said.

"Mom, I need you to sit down."

"Why, what's happened?"

"Neal and I are in the hospital where Christopher is having a CAT scan taken."

"What for?" she asked.

Carole continued, "We have taken him to a neurologist and the doctor thinks he has a brain tumor." Carole heard her suck in that gasp of air that goes with tragic news. "Mom, I am so sorry that I called you with no one there to comfort you, but I just needed to hear your voice. I'm so sorry to call you with bad news but I had to tell you what is going on."

"I'm glad you called. I want you to be strong, darling. Can you be strong for Christopher?"

"I'll try, Mom." Carole told her that we were staying at the hospital with Christopher and that she would try and call her Dad later.

She ended the call by hearing her mother say, "Remember that I love you sweetheart, and please stay in touch. Do you hear me, Carole?"

Carole felt her mother's fear, disbelief, confusion, and love as she spoke a tearful good-bye. She stood there feeling numb and lost. Shortly, I returned to tell her that the scans were over and that Christopher had done well.

We were taken back to the Scottish Rite Children's Hospital. It was so great to see Carole holding him close again. All the priorities in our lives shifted. How precious it is to hug your child, especially when his life hangs in the balance!

I didn't really know what to pray for or even how to pray. My faith had been on the shelf for years. I knew I had to pray to God, but how would I pray? The doctors seemed to have all the facts in their corner, but all we wanted was our precious child diagnosed, treated, and healed. It felt like we were descending into Dante's inferno without even a flicker of light to see our way out. What does a mom or dad do or say at such a time? It would be hours before we would have the results of the CAT scan. After making sure Christopher and Carole were settled into his room, I left to make preparations for his unexpected stay in the hospital.

HOME ALONE—LILBURN, GEORGIA, 1984

Arriving home alone late that afternoon to gather some personal things for Christopher's hospital stay, I anguished with thoughts of what might lie ahead for Carole, Christopher, and for me. I hoped the scan results would be negative. Nevertheless, evaluating the events that had taken place during the two months of Christopher's quarantine and the doctor's suspicions of him having a brain tumor, I feared the worst was about to be revealed.

I took a suitcase from the master bedroom closet shelf, opened it, and placed it on our bed. I then walked down the hall and into Christopher's dark room. A terrifying thought came to me that everything in that room could possibly become just reminders of a little boy whom we loved so dearly. I turned on the light, but a fear filled my mind as I saw his room without him in it.

His pictures hung on the wall and his toys were scattered here and there. With tears blurring my vision, I made my way back to the master bedroom, holding some clothing I'd taken from Christopher's dresser drawer. I was totally numb. Yes, I was moving about and going through the motions, but I was on overload and felt as if I was about to explode.

I folded his pajamas and placed them in the suitcase and then I felt it. An unseen force, like a magnet, suddenly pulled me down to my knees. I fell across the foot of the bed, and from deep within my spirit, I cried out to God, "Please don't let Christopher die!" For years I had not asked much of God. As a matter of fact, I had drifted so far from Him that I hardly prayed at all. In previous years, when I felt the need to pray about something, I would stop and think, *Why bother God with this problem? I can probably handle it myself.*

As long as the doctors could do something to help Christopher during his quarantine, it never occurred to me to talk with God. I struggled with the terrifying thought that our son's life could be taken by a brain tumor, just like my Aunt Dolly's who had died six months earlier of a malignant brain tumor. I remembered that during the months following her doctor's diagnosis, she suffered after brain surgery. She was extremely sick from chemotherapy treatments and endured the shock and embarrassment of losing her hair. She fought a long and courageous battle for her life, but still lost.

Tormenting images of my aunt, lying comatose on a hospital bed, her body swollen from so many steroid medications and water retention, began to flash through my mind. I cried out, "Dear God, please don't let this horrible fate come to Christopher!" I begged and pleaded with God for a long time, and then finally made my way back to the hospital.

I dreaded facing the doctors. I wanted an instant miracle for my child and for all of this to go away. Honestly, no ray of hope penetrated my consciousness. A noted theologian, Reinhold Niebuhr, said some years ago, "Faith is a citadel of hope built on the brink of despair." Driving back to the hospital, I realized that I had so little faith and didn't know where to get it. It's impossible to build a fortress of hope against negative news when the building blocks of faith don't exist.

One thing was certain: I was on the brink of despair. Going over the edge wasn't an option. Every fiber of my being cried out in my despair to God, "Don't let Christopher die! You promised me a seed, a son. I can't make that promise happen. Help me." Sinking into the waves of desperation, I entered the hospital to face the doctors.

My God, My God, Why Have You Forsaken…

Eight o'clock that same evening, Carole and I met with Dr. Schub for the reading of the scan. He pointed to a shadow on the film and said, "Definitely, a brain tumor."

His words hit like a death sentence for a condemned, guilty murderer. But Christopher hadn't done anything wrong. The very people who were supposed to help him were sentencing this beautiful, innocent child. Surely, the doctor could do something. Would he offer any hope?

Dr. Schub explained that it looked as though the tumor was in a position where it could be easily removed. We desperately embraced his evaluation. Brain surgery was a jolting thought for us. We realized how serious it could be. We hoped that the tumor would be benign, and that we had discovered it in time to prevent further damage. Slowly, we retreated from the brink of despair, but our hope would be soon diminished.

Christopher was transferred to Emory's Henrietta Egleston Children's Hospital the following morning and placed in the care of Dr. Mark O'Brian, head of pediatric neuro-surgery. Our hope that the tumor was in a position to be easily removed quickly vanished. Dr. O'Brian said the tumor appeared malignant. The scan indicated that its tentacles had already infiltrated the left side of his brain stem.

Because of the tumor's position, even a biopsy would be very risky. If his brain stem were to be cut accidentally during surgery, Christopher could be terribly maimed or killed. Dr. O'Brian suggested shunt surgery to relieve the pressure in Christopher's head, then radiation treatment. Finally Carole and I were given the diagnosis and prognosis. Christopher was suffering from an inoperable, malignant brain stem tumor, and given, at most, 18 months to live.

Talk about a total shock—we were like walking zombies! Our minds plunged into a dense fog of fear and disbelief. It was as though the evidence had been presented to the doctors who comprised the entire jury. They had deliberated and come to a unanimous conclusion. The verdict was *guilty, in the first degree*. Our son was guilty of having a deadly, incurable disease and his sentence was *death*. He was being sentenced to carry out a short length of time on this earth in a world of painkillers, poking, needles, and prodding. But they would attribute his death to natural causes.

At that moment, something rose up in me and simply screamed, "No!" I looked into Carole's eyes with a conviction and confidence that meant business. "We will not accept this horrible fate for our son. He will live! I don't care what the scan revealed. I will not allow him to lie here in this hospital and die! To accept what we've just heard, 'Malignant brain stem tumor...eighteen months to live... radiation and chemo treatments,' all meaning that Christopher's case will become just another statistic. God *can* and *will* heal Christopher!"

It was imperative that we appeal to a *higher court with an even Higher Power* who would make the final decision. We would plead our case with the only Advocate who gave His life for such causes. Medicine isn't God and doctors cannot play God. They may have the facts, but they don't have two essential compounds for a cure—faith and truth. At the time, I didn't know this, but somewhere inside of me, I knew that the final diagnosis and prognosis were in God's hands, not in ours or the doctors' grasp. So we moved from the darkest of valleys into the only path left for us—faith. We obviously didn't know what that meant; we didn't know how to walk by faith or even how to pray. But like Abram of old, I simply had a promise—Christopher was my promised seed from God. That's all I had; and it had to be enough to see us through.

A VOICE OF TENACITY

It was strange that I started to take a strong stand for God to heal Christopher. Desperation drives us to move in directions we have never traveled before. In the little Baptist church that I had attended as a youth, salvation was the main focus. We were taught that God sent His only begotten Son, Jesus, to die on the cross for our sins. If we accepted Jesus into our hearts as our Lord and Savior, believing He died and was resurrected, we would receive our redemption and eternal life in heaven. I had done that back in those early days but had gotten sidetracked.

I needed to know how to get back on a faith track and also how to move from the natural, medical reports to a good report from God. Later on I would read a passage from

Jeremiah, *"We have heard the report of it; our hands grow feeble"* (Jer. 6:24). But I would also learn the verse from Isaiah that brought faith and comfort to my heart, *"Who has believed our report? And to whom has the arm of the Lord been revealed?"* (Isa. 53:1).

Yes, we were stunned by the doctors' reports and we found ourselves weak and depressed. Still, we had a report from God that our future and our legacy were wrapped up in our son. How could that report not be true? How could our promised seed be facing imminent death? After all, it was not for me or for Carole, but for our little boy who had done no wrong. Somehow, I felt like I was in a war zone! There were some forces unseen that wanted our son to die. I could not see them, touch them, or even explain them except for the fact that I felt their icy presence! In my heart, I knew they existed. They wanted him dead. Their weapons of mass destruction were all aimed at our son. That brought great anxiety and fear because I did not really know what I was fighting against. This realization left me feeling absolutely powerless, and that convinced me even more that I needed to get out of myself and back into God's good graces.

I had never heard any teaching in my church about fighting spiritual battles. What did I have to do? What could I do to receive healing for Christopher? I thought back to my early church days and remembered them praying for people. They prayed, "God, if it be Thy will…."

I decided to start there. I rationalized that God created Christopher for His purpose. Therefore, I could no longer doubt or question His will. I had to believe that God wanted Christopher to live and not die. I wondered if Carole could walk in agreement with me; and I wondered if her parents could understand this out-of-the-box faith stance we had to pursue.

Carole and her family were members of the Reformed Jewish temple. She learned, by reading the prayer book and hearing sermons, how God delivered the Jewish people from the bondage of slavery in Egypt and led them into the Promised Land. She began to question, "Can I reach back through thousands of years to a God who performed such wondrous miracles? Could it be that He will hear my cry for help and have a way provided for my son's deliverance and healing?"

Although many aspects of our religious beliefs were different, we did, however, have common ground. Both of us believed in the one and only true God. We prayed for direction and knew we had to find a ministry and church family that could help us as we sought a miracle healing for Christopher.

As a younger man, I heard the teaching by a renowned minister named Dr. Oral Roberts. He taught about the laying on of hands to heal the sick, anointing with oil, and trusting God for supernatural miracles. He also taught about seed faith; and by believing and _not doubting,_ and speaking to life's mountains, that they could be removed. This was certainly a mountain of monumental size! As a child, these seeds of faith had been sown into my spirit. Now, when I needed them most, they were beginning to grow.

From Christopher's hospital room, we called Oral Roberts University trying to connect with someone who might believe that miracles were possible. It was the first time we reached out for ministry or prayer support. Two days later, a lady from the ministry returned my call. She said our prayer request had reached Dr. Oral Roberts's desk and the prayers were being lifted. I had never heard anyone pray the *prayer of faith*. This wonderful prayer warrior prayed with such power and conviction that I could almost feel the Holy Spirit coming through the telephone line.

Placing the receiver back on the telephone, I turned to face the doctor who had just walked into the room. Although we were about to hear more bad reports, a glimmer of hope had just been sparked within me. I felt that God was hearing our prayers, giving me more assurance that He would heal Christopher. I did not know how or when, but deep inside I just knew that Christopher was going to live and not die. Carole and I had lit a candle in the darkness. The darkness was still there, but the light of life overcomes darkness. A war was raging, but a refuge of peace or *shalom* began to form in each of our hearts. We didn't know the way out of the darkness, but at least we had a candle for the next step. We would need it. The medical reports would not offer any hope.

Chapter 5

FIGHTING FOR OUR LIVES

EMORY'S HENRIETTA EGLESTON HOSPITAL— DECATUR, GEORGIA, DECEMBER 1984

Our battles were now intensifying; our lives were being torn apart. The pleasure we once had in seeing our son enjoying his young life were now mere memories. Christopher had always been a calm, cooperative boy. Now, because of the tremendous pressure in his brain, he would go into uncontrollable rages. We were watching every aspect of his life change, and that change directly affected ours too.

One evening, while trying to settle him into his hospital bed, he experienced a full-blown rage. He screamed and tossed to and fro from the head of the bed to the foot. Then he got out of bed and pushed a wheelchair up and down the hallway. The only way to settle him down was for the nurses to administer sedatives. I don't know which was worse, seeing him angry and out of control or watching the nurses sedate him to calm him into manageable behavior.

The doctor came and explained that the funnel-like area in his head that allows the brain fluid to circulate through the body had been pressed shut because of the tumor's size and location. The ventricles were filled with fluid, causing tremendous pressure and causing his head size to increase. To relieve the pressure in his brain, the doctor suggested shunt surgery.

In Christopher's case, the type of shunt used would have a small catheter, with a short, six-inch liter on one side and long tubing on the other side. The catheter itself would be inserted just beneath his skull. The short liter, with small holes at its end, would be directed into the dead part of his brain. Its function would be to accumulate trapped brain fluid, then feed the fluid through the catheter and allow it to circulate properly through his body. The long tubing would run along his neck and down into his abdominal area, while the tubing's extra length would be coiled at its end to allow for Christopher's future growth.

After the shunt surgery, Christopher was returned to his private room. Carole and I were with him around the clock. During that night, Carole changed his wet night clothing several times. We thought he had been urinating on his gown. But early the next morning, we stood him at the commode and lifted his gown. To our surprise, we found brain fluid draining from the abdominal incision.

Examinations revealed that his body had rejected the shunt. Christopher was scheduled for a second shunt surgery on December 19, 1984. He was always allowed to stay with us until he became drowsy enough so he wouldn't become emotionally upset before taking him to the OR. When the anesthesiologist came to sedate our son, he shared some very disturbing facts. Christopher had an allergic reaction to the anesthesia used during surgery; therefore, a narcotic would be used during the next one. The allergic reaction to the anesthesia caused him to have lockjaw and also brought on symptoms of a very rare muscle disease that is not detectable unless induced. Concerned that Christopher might have this muscle disease, the doctor informed us that if his temperature reached 105 degrees, he might not survive. This disease was so rare that medical research had yet to develop an antidote.

Carole held Christopher in her arms as the anesthesiologist administered the sedative. Our minds drifted back to his birth. Carole recalled the nurse placing him in her arms for the first time. A beautiful gift from God, an event she had waited so long to experience. I remembered holding my son, looking into his face and saying my first "Hello" to him. Could it be that we were saying our last good-bye to Christopher? As he was being wheeled down the long corridor toward the operating room, it felt as though Carole and I were standing helplessly on a deserted beach during a raging storm. The storm's darkness surrounded us.

Filled with anguish and despair, we watched as the undertow and turbulent waves seemed to be taking our only child away from us and further and further out to sea. We had to place him into the arms of the professionals and ultimately into God's care.

Christopher went into surgery and I went back to his room to gather our personal belongings. Because of the possibility of Christopher's temperature rising, he would be monitored in ICU for the next 24 hours. There really wasn't much for a father or mother to do. We felt helpless, alone, and we agonized over the pain our son would feel. Could God give us any vision of what we were about to face?

A VISION WORTH SHARING

I want to present you with Carole's thoughts and experience concerning this time:

> Neal and I watched as Christopher was being wheeled down the hall for his second shunt surgery. My heart became heavy laden and burdened with the thought that this might be the last time I would ever get to see him. It might be the last time I could ever hold him in my arms and love on him. I felt the sunshine of my life was about to go under this cloud of gloom. It would be hard to live life without him. I had been watching his body deteriorate right before my eyes. I felt so helpless.
>
> My sister-in-law Juanita accompanied me to the waiting room. I knelt down before a large window and began to pray, believing God would hear the cry of my heart. I didn't have a personal relationship with Him nor did I know how to pray. I knew God could heal, but my question was: "Would He heal my son?"
>
> I cried out to Juanita, "Look, there's God!" As I began to focus my eyes toward heaven, the clouds began to take shape and I felt that I was taken into another realm—the spirit realm—and there I saw Father God. _"His head and hair were white like_

wool, as white as snow, ...and his countenance was as the sun shineth in his strengths" (Rev. 1:14, 16b).

For that brief moment, God's presence brought me peace, comfort, and assurance that everything was going to be all right. Then I noticed in the background, layer upon layer of clouds forming, and I thought Christopher had died and that was where he was laid to rest—in the presence of the Almighty God. As it was when I had the vision with Neal's father, a reassuring message was given to me. I heard a still small voice in my spirit, saying, "Don't worry, Carole, your son is with Me. I'm holding him safely in My arms."

Surviving the surgery, Christopher returned to us much weaker in body but completely different in spirit. We did not know what happened, but there were very noticeable changes in him. Much later we learned that he had an experience, an encounter that would shape his life forever.

BEYOND THE OPERATING ROOM DOORS

Christopher later shared with Carole and me what happened to him during surgery. He will share it with you now to give you a glimpse of the kind of supernatural atmosphere he found himself in. Here's his account:

> While I was in surgery, I suddenly found myself being carried upward by two angels. The mix of blue skies and white clouds disappeared as we quickly approached a most beautiful and majestic

city. I did not know what I was seeing, but somehow my spirit knew that it was heaven.

When we reached the gates to that city, I saw a Man with long brown hair, wearing a white robe with a purple sash around His waist, standing in the mist; and I knew it was Jesus. When He saw me, He stepped out of the mist, opened the gates, turned toward me, and said, "Welcome to heaven, Christopher." He then took my hand and said, "Come with Me, I want to introduce you to My Father."

Walking down the golden streets together, we came to a big mansion with many stories. Drawing closer, I saw that it seemed to be made of gold. I imagined that it had many rooms—too many to count. Jesus escorted me to my own room. Since my favorite color is purple, I was happy to see that the walls were covered in purple. And there was an inscription that read, "Jesus is Lord."

Entering my room, I saw God sitting at a desk in the corner. There were two objects on the desk: anointing oil and the Lamb's Book of Life. God told me that without these two elements miracles were slim.

Suddenly, as being translated, I found myself standing at the gates of hell with Jesus. He never told me why He took me there. But we stood there in almost total darkness. The only light was an occasional flicker from the flames beyond. Even before entering, I could hear the horrible screams of tortured souls and the stench of burning flesh. Two imp demons met us. They had the most hideous faces that I had ever seen. They opened the gates and took me through. I didn't fear because I knew God's Spirit was with me at all times.

Looking around at various pits, I saw that they were filled with people screaming while demons were laughing and dancing around. Then the two imps led me into Satan's private domain. He was sitting on his throne made of bones with two adult skulls at the top and two baby skulls on the arm rests. He looked like a man with burnt, brown skin. His face was kind of angelic (in a dark, twisted way). There was something cunning about the way he spoke.

"You are *not* going to survive the brain tumor!" Satan hissed at me.

Then, just like before, I was quickly translated back to heaven, present with Jesus. As we walked through a beautiful garden, He told me not to believe the devil's lies. He said, "I have plans for you. I want you to preach to the Jews and Gentiles and have a healing ministry. If you don't obey, the blood of those I have sent to you will be on your hands."

As we continued to walk, I saw a man lying on the ground resting against a large stone. When he heard our footsteps approaching, he looked up at me. It was my Papa! He was surprised to see me there and said, "Christopher, go back to your parents!"

Suddenly, I felt myself floating while being pulled downward. As I entered the hospital room, I saw myself lying on the operating table. Many people, wearing white coats and masks, were frantically working on me. My spirit entered my body as quickly as it had ascended. When I opened my eyes in the ICU, instead of being well and in heaven with Jesus, I found myself again trapped in a sick body. I did not know how to tell anybody about what had just happened to me.

In His Presence—Lilburn, Georgia, December 1984

Christopher was released from the hospital after the second shunt surgery on December 21, 1984. We wanted him to enjoy Christmas as much as possible. So the tree was put up in the living room. In order for him to help with the decorating, I held him up to the tree and assisted him with hanging the ornaments. His eyes danced with excitement as he watched the bright lights. However, it was difficult trying to celebrate the birth of God's only Son while faced with the possible death of our own.

Christopher was on heavy doses of steroids. The adverse effects were dreadful. His body swelled terribly. We were told the steroids robbed his body of carbohydrates, causing him to have feelings of constant hunger. When placing food before him, he would grab at it like a wild, starving child. Seeing our son suffering was almost unbearable for us. Frustrations mounted as we prayed for a touch from God. We were still seeking a ministry to lay hands on Christopher, one that would stand with us in faith for a supernatural healing.

Our old life had moved so fast and become so unrec-
ognizable that we really felt like we were on steroids as
well. In the month of November 1984, the second month
of Christopher's quarantine, I had purchased the assets of
Kome Hair Design, owned by Faye Cleveland and Patsy
Cochran. Since our move back to Georgia in September, I
had worked in a hair salon long enough to obtain a few cli-
ents and felt this was an opportunity to own my own salon
again. We paid cash to buy the business' assets, leaving
a modest balance in an account until we were financially
stable again. We had the new business only one week
when we learned of Christopher's brain tumor. I turned
my back on it and walked away. I knew, without a doubt,
my full attention and support would have to go to Carole
and Christopher.

It seemed as though God preordained our steps to meet
Faye and Patsy. I shared with them about Christopher's illness and of our desire to find a ministry that would believe
he could be healed, even laying hands[1] on him and believing
with us for his healing. Faye extended an invitation for us to
visit her church, River of Life, located in Lilburn, Georgia.
She knew I had been raised in a conservative Baptist church
and Carole in a Reformed Jewish temple. Being concerned
that we might feel a little awkward and uncomfortable in
a charismatic setting, she said, "Don't come just because I
invited you. Please pray that you will be led by the Holy
Spirit to attend the service."

Being that Carole was raised in a Jewish household, my
talk about Jesus was foreign to her. I want you to hear Carole describe her feelings at this critical junction in our walk

together in faith, beginning to believe in this hopeless situation that there might be hope for Christopher to live.

At this important pivotal point of my life, I have to admit that my personal faith had been a bit bumpy. I really did not just glide into this adult life and gently land here. There were some edge-of-your-seat moments and some white-knuckle, hold-on-for-dear-life moments, but I have to share some details so that you can see why this day was so unique.

I had begun to talk with God from the fourth grade. Being a shy, skinny girl with straight hair that wouldn't even curl did not give me a strong or positive self-image. I did not enjoy school, let alone schoolwork, and I had some real struggles trying to explain anything.

Unfortunately, I started comparing myself to my older sister Terry, who was three years my senior. I admired her beauty, social skills, and the way she excelled in everything she did. She was an achiever and very outspoken, the very opposite of me.

Feeling that I was living in her shadow, as others were expecting me to measure up, I struggled to find myself for many years. Instead of taking the school bus home, I would walk, sometimes with classmates, but more often by myself. It was during those times that I began talking to God. I never seemed to get any answers, but I kept sharing, hoping that God was listening. Sometimes, when I arrived home, Nette, my parent's housekeeper, sensed my struggles and would listen to me. When we were alone, she would share about Jesus. I listened with moderate interest. Back then, her comments did not make much sense to me. However, as I know now, the words she spoke were seeds being planted in my spirit.

The war inside of me raged on, and I would ask God questions like, "Why did You ever let me be born? What is Your purpose for me on this earth? Why does life have to hurt so much?" There were so many times that I would tell Him, "I wish I was dead. Please take me out of here!" But He never did and I never really got my questions answered either.

One afternoon after a really bad day at school, I contemplated cutting my wrist, thinking maybe I would bleed to death and my struggles would be over. It's strange how the enemy tries to abolish the plans God has for our future. I know now that it was the protection of my guardian angel that stopped me that day.

Even though I seemed to be talking with God, I didn't *know* Him. You can chat with someone and share all kinds of things but still not call them a personal friend. That was me. I was just chatting, venting, and asking questions. Rarely did I listen. I had not taken that important leap of faith to believe God would take care of me. He was actually listening, understanding, and loving me unconditionally, just as I was.

I was raised in a Reformed Jewish home with wonderful and unselfish parents who loved me and made sacrifices for my sisters and me. Their love really touched my heart and shaped my life. We attended temple on the High Holy Days. I loved hearing the sound of the Shofar (a ram's horn that is blown, signifying a call to worship). The Rabbi would read passages from the Torah and then deliver his message. At the end of the service, the congregation bowed their heads and closed their eyes as the Rabbi prayed: *"The LORD bless thee, and keep thee: The LORD make His face shine upon thee, and be gracious unto thee: The LORD lift up His countenance upon thee and give thee peace* (Num. 6:24-26 KJV)." I kept my eyes opened to observe the Rabbi. As he raised his arms to pray, his prayer shawl spread as the wings of an angel, touching my heart. As moving as the services were, when leaving the temple I sometimes felt a desire to know more about God.

Friday night dinners were special. It was our Sabbath night together so there was no homework, no commitments with friends, and Dad didn't work that night. A special time was set apart for just family. It kept us all connected. Even today my family remains close. There was, however, something missing. I heard many stories and celebrated many holidays, but I still had never connected in a personal relationship with my heavenly Father. For some reason, my ears were deaf to God's voice and my eyes were blind to His Word. I truly wanted to know God—not just know about Him.

I got involved in activities that I enjoyed in middle school and made many friends, but emptiness lived in my heart. My search to find the truth about God did not go away, however. My parents completed the building of our house in the Baltimore County area. It was just in time for me to start high school; it was a positive move for me and I started a new season in life. I got my driver's license, which gave me independence. I went out for sports (basketball and softball), and that helped to release some of my unbridled hyperactivity. Sports involvement allowed me to mingle with people of varied faiths, both Jewish and Christian. I distinctly remember coming home one afternoon from school and announcing to my mom, "When, and if I ever get married, it will be to a non-Jewish man." She didn't say anything or ask any questions. Maybe she thought this too would pass. I really don't know why I said it, but from that day on I started to become more outspoken.

After graduation, I went into junior college in Pennsylvania to take merchandising. My dad had a furniture business and I helped out some there. I loved meeting and helping people and I enjoyed the constant activity of moving around and not sitting in one place. My dad and I were alike in some ways. We even watched some television preachers like Jimmy Swaggart and Billy Graham together. I always felt he had a desire within his heart to know more about God just as I did. He was brought up in the Orthodox temple while my mom was brought up in the Reformed temple where the services spoke more English and families sat together.

College was a good experience for me. After graduation, I gained lots of hands-on experience in my area of study. I worked in Baltimore for five-and-a-half years with a boss that became the best mentor in my life—besides my parents, of course. About four years into the job, I became sick and the doctor didn't know what was wrong with me. My fever began to rise quickly and they thought they should take me to the hospital. I was a little concerned when Nette mixed some onions, garlic, and herbs together, made a paste and wrapped the poultice around my neck. She prayed over me in Jesus's name. I believe she was a prayer warrior for me. It worked and my fever broke. It took some time but I regained my strength.

More than anything else in the world, I wanted Jesus now to be the Great Physician for Christopher. Jesus told His disciples after they questioned Him about why they couldn't deliver a demonized boy, *"Because you have so little faith. I tell you the truth, if you have faith as small as a mustard seed, you can say to this mountain, 'Move from here to there' and it will move. Nothing will be impossible for you"* (Matt. 17:20 NIV).

The seeds about Jesus that Nette had planted in me years ago were now taking root and beginning to grow. I wanted to believe Jesus could heal Christopher; but *would* He? As I sat in the pew that day at River of Life Church, what a revelation I received. My entire life had prepared me for this moment. It was now time to make a decision. I would have to decide if I *could* trust Him or if I even *would* trust Him—no matter what!

Now you have a picture of what was happening inside of Carole during this time. What we both faced was unfamiliar spiritual territory, a growing awareness of spiritual warfare, and a battle for Christopher's life that was going from intense to horrific!

ENDNOTE

1. We had read a passage in the New Testament that gave us some hope: James 5:14-15 reads, *"Is anyone among you sick? Let him call for the elders of the church, and let them pray over him, anointing him with oil in the name of the Lord. And the prayer of faith will save the sick, and the Lord will raise him up. And if he has committed sins, he will be forgiven."*

Chapter 6

DOES ANYONE HAVE
ANY ANSWERS?

LILBURN, GEORGIA, DECEMBER 1984

Carole and I felt we needed more than a *if-this-is-God's-will* type of religion. Let me explain what I mean by this. It was one thing for both of us to believe that God existed. Jews, Christians, Muslims, Deists, and many others believe that. For us, simply knowing that God was "out there" wasn't enough. He had to get involved in our lives, in our personal crises, right here and right now. We needed people who believed that God performed miracles today just as He had in the past for Abraham, Moses, Elijah, Peter, and Paul. Just reading about or hearing about those miracles, those interventions of God, were not enough for us. A distant God doesn't work when your three-year-old son is facing death from a cancerous tumor! Did anyone believe in a present, upfront, in-your-face God who acted now in time and space and actually healed people?

After some time of consideration we accepted Faye's invitation. We felt this church with our newfound friends could be an answer to our prayers and hoped their faith in God held the hope we had been seeking. On December 23, 1984, Faye greeted us in the foyer of River of Life Church. We had taken Christopher from his bed, still wrapped in a blanket, with his hair tangled and his head scarred from shunt surgeries. The congregation was already singing as we entered the sanctuary. Many languages were spoken in unknown tongues. The atmosphere was electrified with loud rhythmic music. A few people were dancing in the aisles, their hands lifted as they worshiped. Coming from a conservative Baptist background, this was a spiritual culture shock for me as well as Carole with her Jewish background. Although these things were foreign to both of us, we were determined to keep our minds focused on the purpose of our visit. God was still in the business of performing miracles and we really needed one for our son.

Faye led us to the right of the church, seating us on the aisle in the third pew from the front. My emotions vacillated back and forth between hope and desperation. It was such a strange balancing act! Christopher was very calm as we entered the sanctuary and he remained amazingly calm throughout the entire service. There was a hope that was beginning to rise up within my heart. Maybe my desperation was impatience. I wanted Christopher to be well right *now*, with no more painful surgeries.

Christopher lay in my arms as we listened to the congregation sing, "Reach Out and Touch the Lord as He Passes By." How appropriate that song was as we were attempting to touch the hem of Jesus's garment in the spiritual realm, just as the woman with the issue of blood did when He walked the earth (see Matt. 9:20-21).

The church ushers passed the offering plate for the morning tithes and offerings. I filled out the first-time visitor's card and dropped it in the plate as it passed by. The card had a question written on it: "What do you need the Lord to do for you?" I wrote, "I need God's healing for our son's brain tumor." The request was brought to Pastor Bob Wright.

Carole, Christopher, and I were called to the front of the church. Pastor Wright asked that we let our requests be known to God and to call up the elders of the church (as instructed in James 5:14-15). After anointing Christopher with oil, Pastor Wright and the elders cursed the root of the tumor to die in the name of Jesus. He asked God to heal Christopher and restore strength and life into his weak and dying body. With mixed emotions, we turned to leave the pulpit, encountering the awesome presence of God through the congregation. They were all standing to their feet. Their hands were lifted toward heaven, agreeing with us that Christopher would be healed (see Matt. 18:19-20). Salvation was offered later to those who felt led of the Holy Spirit to receive. Carole accepted her Messiah, Jesus, as her Lord and Savior that day.

I rededicated my life to the Lord during the same service out of personal necessity. I had drifted away from my first love and had become entangled with the world. After my initial salvation experience, I had not persisted with a tenacious faith. I had lived a self-centered life that was not pleasing to God. Even during the hard times in my earlier rough years, I did not turn to the Lord.

When people and natural means could do nothing more for my son, I knew my back was against the wall. With no other options to save Christopher's life, I sought his Creator.

God pulled me down to my knees in prayer. That is what I call a total surrender. What an awesome God who would give His Son so that *my* son might live.

Before leaving the church, we met a man and his wife, Jerald and Patsy Joiner. Jerald was serving as an elder of the church and Patsy taught Sunday school and assisted in office duties. They recognized our great need for counsel in God's Word, to learn how to stand and claim healing for Christopher.

We left River of Life Church with a sense of disappointment that Christopher had not received an instantaneous healing. We looked at him, hoping to see some improvement in his condition. Unfortunately, there was none to be seen. In fact, he grew even worse. In our hearts we knew for sure that something positive had happened, but our eyes were seeing something quite different.

The good part was that now Carole and I were equally yoked in our Christian faith. We would stand together strengthened by the power of the Holy Spirit to fight against the enemy that had come to kill, steal, and destroy our family (see John 10:10).

Patsy was sympathetic to Carole's needs. She began to put together a support group of ladies in the church to assist us with our everyday needs. Many times she, Jerald, and others would be available throughout the day or night, giving us prayer support and assuring us that Christopher would not die. They encouraged us that God would work in our lives in His time and His way. Those faithful saints began teaching us how to speak the Scriptures and how to wield *"the sword of the Spirit, which is the word of God"* (Eph. 6:17) to defeat our enemies—Satan, disease, and death.

The Bible tells us, *"So then faith comes by hearing, and hearing by the word of God"* (Rom. 10:17). Carole and I felt a need to return to church and receive the teachings of God's Word. Two weeks after our initial visit to the church, Patsy encouraged us to come again, saying she would take care of Christopher while we attended service. As Pastor Bob Wright prayed that morning, he shared that he felt he had received a message from God or a word of knowledge: "Christopher will live and not die!"

FACING THE DARKNESS

In the coming months, this declaration often became our only ray of hope. We were encouraged by these words and felt God was moving in our circumstances.

During mid-service, Carole insisted I check in on Christopher. Patsy was teaching Sunday school for the three- and four-year-old children. When I entered the classroom, my heart was touched by what I saw. Patsy was holding Christopher on her lap as the little children prayed for him. She said he had been sick and had regurgitated. By the time we left the service, Christopher was feeling much better. He said to us, "I'm hungry. I want to go to Wendy's." We took him there and fed him as much as he could eat.

Returning home, he took an unusually long nap. When we heard him awakening, Carole and I rushed into the bedroom. We were always anticipating a positive change in his condition, trusting that we would soon witness a miraculous healing. I lay beside Christopher as Carole stood at the bedside. I said to him, "I'm glad you're finally awake, I miss you when you sleep so long."

Christopher looked at me and said, "When I was in the womb…"

"What did you say?" I asked.

"When I was in the womb," he repeated.

"I don't know what that means," I answered.

He then said, "Before I was born, I wondered what your name was."

"Christopher, you're saying you wondered who I was even before you were born. Did you know your mother?"

"Yes," he replied, "I knew Mom."

It was 5:30 p.m. when he awoke. Carole and I were absolutely stunned. We wondered what could compel our son to say such strange things. I wrote down exactly the words Christopher had said and placed the notation in my armoire. It was 5:30 p.m. on January 7th, 1985.

At 3:00 a.m. the next morning, Christopher awakened sick and vomiting. As Carole placed a cool, wet washcloth on his face, he looked at me and said, "The germ in my body that's making me sick is named Adra."

Startled, I turned to Carole and asked, "What is he saying?"

"I don't know!" she replied.

The atmosphere in the room quickly changed. It felt as if we were standing in the very presence of evil. My mind labored trying to respond to what we had just heard. The Holy Spirit quickened me that a demonic spirit was attacking our child. I placed my hand on Christopher's head, tried to recall what Pastor Wright and the elders had done when they cursed the root of the tumor and commanded it to die. With all the strength and faith I could muster, I said, "God rebuke you, Adra, in the name of Jesus! I command you to leave Christopher's body right now!"

Now we had the name of the demonic spirit that sought to kill Christopher. While the hosts of heaven gathered to battle on Christopher's behalf, the hoards of hell gathered to snuff out his life. I continued to rebuke Adra in the name of Jesus Christ. From ancient days of Eastern Orthodoxy, Christians from the first century until today have rebuked the works of the devil. With the heavenly hosts of angels and the cloud of witnesses (see Heb. 12), I now entered the fray. How little I understood what was happening.

BEGINNING TO WALK BY FAITH

Initially, when all this first started, we could only see the physical aspects of Christopher's illness. They were horrible to watch and they were even more painful and dehumanizing for Christopher to endure. However, our eyes were now being opened to an entirely new dimension. We were suddenly being thrust into an unfamiliar realm where we were warring in the spirit world and battling with an unseen adversary.

Suffering from worry and lack of sleep, our minds were being overloaded due to the unusual things that were happening so quickly. We had never heard Christopher mention the word *womb* before. And it was baffling to hear him name a germ in his body that was making him sick.

While we did not understand the spiritual realities facing us, we wanted to support Christopher in every way possible. It's amazing the strength one is given by God and the boldness that arises when needed to battle, whether it be in the natural or the spiritual realm. By having Christopher speak these profound things, I felt God was revealing to us the true battle we were to fight.

One afternoon, a member from the church came for a visit and to inquire about Christopher. As we were sharing, he pointed his finger at me and said, "Neal, it is your fault that your son is dying. You have been disobedient to the call of the Lord in your life."

I could only wonder if this statement could be true. Carole and I had asked many times, "What have we done to cause this horrible thing to happen to our child?" We wished to take his illness on ourselves rather than putting Christopher through the hell he was experiencing. It took some time, but I learned what the Bible says about our afflictions: *"These trials are only to test your faith, to see whether or not it is strong and pure"* (1 Pet. 1:7 TLB). The statement that was made by a well-meaning church member was nothing short of pure legalism. Nevertheless, God used that accusation to encourage me to turn to Him in prayer, to seek answers and guidance.

Joni Griggs, the wife of the associate pastor of the River of Life Church, was sitting with Christopher while Carole ran out to do some shopping. Joni said to me, "Neal, why don't you go into the guest room and try to rest while Christopher is sleeping."

As I lay there, praying and seeking God, I thought about what had been said to me. In a silent prayer, I said, "Father, if it is true that I have been disobedient in doing Your will for my life, please reveal to me what You want of me. Lord, I am willing to do anything if You will only heal our son." What happened next did not make any sense to me at all.

Being that I knew very little about the Bible, especially the Old Testament, it seemed strange that the name Jeremiah came to my mind. I did not even know such a book in the Bible even existed. When I began to think of Jeremiah 1:26, I couldn't conceive that this might be the voice of the Lord speaking to me. I dismissed the thought and considered it to be just a trick of my imagination.

Unable to rest, I got out of bed and walked into the living room. Unexpectedly, the Scriptures from Jeremiah came to my thoughts again. I finally walked over and picked up the large Bible that had been given to us as a wedding gift. Flipping through the pages, I was surprised to discover there was indeed a book written about a prophet named Jeremiah. I thought, *This will be rather simple. I'll read Jeremiah 1:26.* Discovering there were only 19 verses in the first chapter, I asked the Lord, "Did I misunderstand?" There was no answer, only an unsettling silence. Staring at the opened Bible placed before me on the dining room table, I listened carefully, hoping to hear that still small voice that had just previously spoken to me.

Again, there was total silence. Without having clarity of the Scriptures I was to read, I considered it might have been chapter 1 through 26 instead. Continuing to read, I began to realize what the prophet Jeremiah was doing. He was telling the people of the nations what God had commanded him to say. Suddenly, I was engulfed by the awesome presence of the Holy Spirit. Warm salty tears flowed down my cheeks and dropped from my face onto the pages of the Bible. I was slammed by the thought that God might be revealing in His written Word what He wanted me to do.

Just an hour before, I bargained with Him, promising to do anything He wanted if He would heal Christopher. The silence was suddenly broken by the resonate tones of my own voice making a quick retort, "God, I can't do this! I don't even know who You are! I could never talk to people about You. I wouldn't know what to say!"

I didn't realize until much later what I told the Lord was similar to what had been said by Jeremiah: *"Then said I: 'Ah, Lord God! Behold, I cannot speak, for I am a youth'"* (Jer. 1:6).

Perhaps the Lord had a dual purpose in having me read these passages in the book of Jeremiah: first, to encourage me to be bold in my witness for Him and, second, to have me parallel these Scriptures with the mind-boggling statements Christopher had made. Carole and I had wondered what the purpose was for him speaking such strange things and had pondered their origin.

God said to Jeremiah, *"Before I formed thee in the belly, I knew thee"* (Jer. 1:5 KJV) Christopher had said to me, "Before I was born, I wondered what your name was." Although God's statement to Jeremiah and what Christopher had said to me were opposite, I felt there might be a connection. But what? Then, Jeremiah 1:9 really grabbed my attention. *"Then the Lord put forth His hand, and touched my mouth. And the Lord said unto me, Behold, I have put my words in thy mouth"* (KJV).

Had God put His words in Christopher's mouth, as He had done in Jeremiah's? That led me to question even more: "Since Jeremiah was a prophet, could it be that God had a similar call on Christopher's life?"

My mind was racing! I just could not seem to read enough or get enough answers. Between trips to the hospital and camping out in Christopher's room, I felt like I had become a Bible bookworm. Just when I had one question answered, it would take me down a new path. Every twist and turn built my faith. God had brought Christopher into the world not just as a promised seed to perpetuate our family name, but to be a light in darkness for others who would face the hellish attacks of the enemy seeking to steal, kill, and destroy. A much greater purpose for Christopher's life and ours began to emerge. I was awed. Needless to say, hell was infuriated and the worst attacks were yet to come.

TESTED FAITH—EMORY'S HENRIETTA EGLESTON HOSPITAL— DECATUR, GEORGIA 1985

The pressure in Christopher's brain continued to increase. The shunt wasn't working. A third shunt surgery was done at Emory's Henrietta Egleston Hospital on January 11th, 1985.

Christopher's body had begun to reject the shunt that was inserted during the previous surgery. Therefore, Dr. O'Brian felt it necessary to remove the tubing from the abdominal area and feed it directly into his heart. Worry and anxiety began to mount as Carole and I waited anxiously for Christopher to come out of the operating room. To put it very plainly, we were nearing our wits' end.

Christopher was again placed in intensive care. Only one person at a time was allowed to visit him for five minutes each hour. In the waiting room, we watched the evening news reporter as he told a story of a young boy that had been brutally injured and had been taken to Egleston Hospital. To my surprise, when I went back to visit Christopher, the little boy I had just heard about on television was in the bed next to his. The privacy curtain was pulled around Christopher's bed to shield him from so much commotion in the ICU. The doctors and nurses were working franticly to save the life of another child in the room next to his.

Pushing the curtain aside to enter where Christopher lay, I was even more horrified to discover his hands and feet were tethered to the bed rails. He was in a state of panic, rising up from his pillow as much as he could, crying, "Mom! Mom! Mom!" With all my being, I so desperately wanted to release him from his shackles, take him into my arms, and run to safety. But I knew, as heartbreaking as it was, this procedure was necessary. While not an easy task or completely success-ful, I calmed Christopher then returned to the waiting room to have Carole go to his bedside. The pressure in his brain caused bouts of uncontrollable rage and no one ever knew when it would happen or exactly what he would do during each episode.

By the grace of God, we made it through that very trying evening. Totally exhausted, we both fell asleep on the couch in a darkened waiting room. At 2:00 a.m., a nurse rushed into the room calling out our name, saying, "Dr. O'Brian needs to see you immediately!" We feared the worst had hap-pened and our child had died.

Dr. O'Brian informed us that an emergency operation was necessary to save Christopher's life. The tubing leading from the shunt feeding into his heart was affecting Christopher's heart valve. Carole asked to see Christopher but the doctor said that would be impossible. He and the nurse turned and disappeared through a door leaving us standing in a deserted hallway in the wee hours of the morning. We really did not know if our child was alive or dead. Carole and I frantically paced the halls. We were relieved when the doctor came out of the OR and said, "Christopher's condition is stable." He added, "I don't know why you won't at least *try* radiation."

We both replied quickly and gave him a definitive, "No."

"It's your choice," he said. "I'm sorry, but no matter what you do, your son can't live much longer." When he finished giving us his report, he turned and walked away, leaving us standing in that hallway, our emotions totally spent.

The fourth shunt surgery seemed to be successful, allowing the brain fluid to flow properly. However, because of the position of the tumor, each operation performed put more pressure on the brain stem and caused Christopher to lose substantial body functions and muscle control. It broke our hearts to see him decline more and more each day.

We were growing in God's Word and still praying for a miracle while doing everything we could think to do in the natural to help Christopher. All we saw was his rapid deterioration. Our families suffered along with us. It appeared to them that the only thing we were doing was keeping him comfortable. My sister Juanita once exclaimed, "Neal, you just can't let Christopher lay there and die! You have to do something!"

I tried to explain through my tears, "We have done all we know to do. The doctors say there is nothing more they can do medically. We have to keep our trust in the Lord. *Christopher is not going to die.* God is going to heal him." By proclaiming the written Word of God and standing stead-fastly on His promises, I believed we would witness the miraculous. Christopher would live and give all glory and honor to his Lord and Savior Jesus Christ. But the question was, *When?*

Chapter 7

New Hope

ATLANTA, GEORGIA AND ABBOTTSVILLE, PENNSYLVANIA, JANUARY 1985

Patsy Joiner had an acquaintance named Joyce Knapton. And one day she shared Joyce's personal testimony with us. Joyce had been diagnosed as having incurable cancer. Her doctors recommended a radical hysterectomy and chemotherapy treatment, for there seemed to be no other alternative in the medical arena. Joyce did research with hopes of discovering other options. She located, and was later admitted to a clinic in Florida headed by Dr. Carey Reams.

Dr. Reams was a biochemist who developed and perfected a technique to test and treat terminally ill patients through nutrition using a biological theory of ionization and nutrition. Dr. Reams was also a Christian who believed in praying for the sick. With the treatment she received at the Reams Clinic and trusting God for healing, Joyce was given a clean bill of health. She became cancer free and had no reoccurrence.

Patsy told us that Joyce studied under Dr. Reams. Now, she too was having success, helping people by using the same techniques and treatments. After much prayer and consideration, we decided to make an appointment with Joyce. We had never heard of the nutritional concept for healing but were eager to try anything that might give Christopher a fighting chance to live.

Carole, Christopher, and I met with Joyce in her home. She made us feel very much at ease with her gentle way and loving manner. She asked me some very pointed questions about Christopher. I especially remember her asking what side of the brain stem the tumor was located. When I told her it was the left side, Joyce's expression went blank and her eyes widened as she looked into mine. She shared later that she realized with the tumor on the left side, Christopher had little chance of survival without a supernatural intervention. The results of Joyce's testing were not promising. There was only a minute chance that nutrition could help, but we were willing to try.

Carole rushed from store to store, buying the necessary juicer, food, and nutritional supplements to begin Christopher's nutritional program. Though mentally and physically exhausted, she proceeded with every ounce of energy she could find. Several days passed and no evidence of a positive change could be seen in our son. As a matter of fact, Christopher's condition was declining even more rapidly. Because of the size of the tumor, the pressure on Christopher's brain stem had affected his equilibrium, rendering him helpless to sit or stand on his own. Carole and I carried our little boy's limp body from room to room, placing pillows around him to support his body. The paralysis had also affected Christopher's ability to speak clearly, making it difficult for him to verbalize and to communicate. It became more difficult to get food and liquid into his body. The small amount he was able to swallow would often result in regurgitation. It was heartbreaking and very obvious that we were standing face to face with the dark spirit of death. We cried out, "God, please help us!"

Joyce suggested that we might consider talking with Dr. Reams about Christopher, thinking perhaps he could encourage us in some way. It had been many years since Joyce had been in contact with Dr. Reams, but was able to locate him in Abbottsville, Pennsylvania. He had semi-retired but continued to treat terminally ill patients on a very limited basis. The love he had for his work and his compassion for people inspired him to continue even into his advanced years.

After speaking with Dr. Reams personally by phone and giving him specifics of Christopher's conditions, he graciously agreed to see us if we could get him to his home in Pennsylvania.

At a point of desperation, we asked ourselves, "Are we just merely grasping for straws, or is the Holy Spirit guiding us?" Conformation was soon given through God's Word: *"Ask, and it will be given to you; seek, and you will find; knock, and it will be opened to you"* (Matt. 7:7). Another door of opportunity had been opened to seek help for Christopher. But would he survive the long trip? Carole and I prayed and agreed we must trust God and walk through the opened door.

I called the Atlanta airport and reserved an early morning flight to Baltimore, Maryland. We made arrangements to be met at the Baltimore/Washington International Airport by Carole's sister and brother-in-law, Sandy and Mike Snitzer.

They volunteered to drive us to Abbottsville, Pennsylvania. An attendant at the Atlanta airport brought a wheelchair down to assist Carole and Christopher to our gate. As we walked the long corridors, my mind drifted back to happier times when Christopher, Carole, and I would travel together. I thought of Christopher as he was then: a happy, energetic, normal little boy, able to run and play, like any other child.

While waiting to board the plane, I couldn't help but notice the sympathetic stares from the other travelers. My heart broke as I looked at Christopher in his mother's arms. She was feeding him water with an eyedropper. Due to the left side of his body being paralyzed, his throat muscles were affected which made it difficult for him to swallow. During our near hour-and-a-half flight, Carole held Christopher on her lap and tried to get more liquids into him.

It was a typical cold but clear day when we arrived at the airport in Baltimore. Mike and Sandy greeted us at our arrival gate. Sandy had traveled to Georgia with her mother and sister, Terry, to visit during the onset of Christopher's illness. She was astonished to see how rapidly his condition had declined. A wheelchair was again necessary to assist Carole and Christopher. We made our way along the long corridors to baggage pickup. Mike and I loaded the luggage while Sandy helped Carole get settled in the backseat with Christopher.

Everything went smoothly during our two-hour drive. We arrived early in the afternoon and were all surprised as we approached a very quaint red brick house located in the rural area of Abbottsville. I remember Sandy commenting, "This is it?" I knew exactly the way she and Mike must have felt.

There is no doubt they thought we had lost our minds to bring Christopher to a place like this. The important thing was that they loved us enough to assist and support us in our decision. We asked Sandy and Mike to keep Christopher in the car while we went in to meet with Dr. Reams.

A gentleman greeted us at the front door, and then escorted us into the living room. There, we were introduced to Dr. Carey Reams. After sharing with him in detail about Christopher's illness and his current condition, he asked us to please bring Christopher into the house. We hugged Mike and Sandy, thanked them, said our good-byes, and promised to keep in touch. Our attention immediately turned back to Dr. Reams and Christopher. A saliva and urine specimen was taken almost immediately. The biochemical testing began.

Because of our emergency situation, Dr. Reams agreed to see Christopher on very short notice. Therefore, the normal facilities were not available. Dr. Reams's wife was very accommodating as she showed us to a small bed located at the top of the stairs in the attic part of the house. We shared the attic area with two other patients at either end of the large room. There were upright screens dividing the sleeping quarters.

Carole and I sat beside Christopher's bed in the dimly lit area attempting to get more liquids into him. We felt so alone and uneasy. We had traveled nearly 800 miles from our home in Georgia desperately seeking anything that could help Christopher. Other than our brief experience with Joyce Knapton and hearing the testimony of her healing, we knew nothing about, nor did we understand, the concept of biochemical treatment through nutrition. At this point we realized we were definitely "out on a limb."

After sharing dinner with the other patients and the clinic's staff, Dr. Reams gave us the results from Christopher's first testing. He was highly toxic, chemically imbalanced, and in a very serious weakened condition. Periodic testing would continue with hopes of seeing a positive change.

Carole and I returned to put Christopher down for the night. As we sat beside his bed, praying and reading Scripture, we noticed his breathing was becoming heavier and more labored. Dr. Reams examined him and then advised us to go immediately to the emergency room at the nearest hospital. When we heard the words *hospital* and *emergency room*, a wave of fear gripped us. One of the male patients and his son volunteered to drive us to the hospital.

We quickly wrapped Christopher in a blanket to protect him from the cold winter night. On the way to the hospital, his breathing became even more severely labored. He began to kick and gasp for breath. All we could do was pray and try to console him. By the time we arrived at the hospital, he had calmed down considerably. Carole and I had a great concern the ER doctors might think that we were not good parents because we had traveled with our sick son so far from our home in Georgia. We couldn't tell them we were at the Reams Clinic because the FDA did not recognize his type of treatment. We prayed that Christopher's vital signs would be normal and that he would be released to go home. We were amazed that Christopher's breathing had returned to normal. We couldn't identify the angel wearing a white lab coat that night, but we felt he was there personally attending to our son.

When we returned to Dr. Reams's house, Mrs. Reams had arranged sleeping accommodations in the living room for better ventilation. She showed such loving compassion for Christopher, playing soothing bedtime music. She sat on the floor and massaged his feet in an attempt to relax him. It was a very long, uneasy, and tense night as we kept a close eye on Christopher.

The next morning Dr. Reams came in early to check on him. He sat down, closed his eyes, and began praying for God's direction. He then told us he believed the Lord was saying to get Christopher to the children's center at the Johns Hopkins Hospital in Baltimore, Maryland.

While Christopher was in Egleston Hospital, his physician sent a copy of his scan to Johns Hopkins for a second opinion. The opinion was the same, which read "totally inoperable" and "no hope for survival." Therefore, Carole and I thought it futile to take Christopher there. Now, with Dr. Reams's prompting, we reconsidered.

BOLD TENACITY—ABBOTTSVILLE, PENNSYLVANIA, JANUARY 1985

We believed that our encounter with Dr. Reams was all part of God's plan. While the entire thing sounded a little unprofessional and far out, you will step outside of the comfort zone and grasp at straws to try to save your child's life. To others this looked impossible and unwise, but to us we felt that God had directed us to Dr. Reams, so who were we to question?

I was even more determined to fight this battle for the life of our son but I also thought about the toll it was taking on

Carole and me. Neither of us slept and we had no appetite. If we slept, Christopher might die before we awoke. Yes, our thinking was irrational but his illness was too! We had no interest in talking to anyone but one another and talking to God about our son.

We tried to let God's Word sustain us. It became our spiritual food and our bodily nourishment. We were novices at this faith walk, but the more we trusted God, the more tenacity we displayed to continue our quest.

I called Johns Hopkins Hospital and spoke with a doctor in the children's center, informed him of the diagnosis we received in Atlanta, of the four shunt surgeries, and Christopher's current condition. I told him that my wife and I believed in God's healing and had traveled to Pennsylvania to seek treatments through biological theory of ionization and nutrition. I told him that now we had been advised to bring our son to Johns Hopkins Hospital. His response to what I told him was abrupt and very rude: "We deal here in reality and clinical facts, not some pie-in-the-sky fantasy about healing through nutrition." His words were hard, cold, and disheartening. Nonetheless, I realized that we had run out of options. So we asked Mike to pick us up and take us to his home in Reisterstown, Maryland. From there we would make arrangements for Christopher's admittance to the Johns Hopkins Hospital.

Dr. Reams continued testing Christopher. Due to the many medications and his lack of liquids and food intake, he had become constipated and more dehydrated. Dr. Reams had the chef prepare a special watermelon juice enema. He said not only would this help Christopher eliminate, but it would also help replenish moisture into his intestines.

All during our quest for a miracle, God was always faithful to send us His vessels with encouragement. As we were working with Christopher, Pat, a former employee of the Reams Clinic, was introduced to us. She said hello and left the room. A few minutes later, Mrs. Reams came in to say that Pat felt compelled to pray for Christopher. She asked for our consent. To have more privacy, we were escorted to a guest bedroom. Pat began to share how the Holy Spirit impressed on her early that morning to visit with Dr. Reams. The small still voice of the Lord said to her, "Someone there is in desperate need of prayer." When she saw Christopher, she knew he was the one.

We laid Christopher on the bed and placed a pillow under his head to position him comfortably. He was very lethargic; his complexion was ashen and pale. While Pat prayed, Christopher seemed to revitalize, as if the Holy Spirit had released energy into his body. A tinge of color flushed his face, his beautiful blue eyes brightened, and he gave us a faint little smile. There is no doubt that the prayers, sent up by the saints of God, were helping to sustain Christopher, imparting renewed strength, giving him a fighting chance for life.

Shortly after Pat prayed, Christopher began to feel the efforts of the watermelon juice enema. His body began to release toxins through excessive vomiting and diarrhea. Another test was taken, but there was very little change in his biochemical balance. Dr. Reams was concerned that Christopher's body was becoming more dehydrated. He urged us to get as much liquid into him as possible.

This was Christopher's fourth birthday! Exactly two years had passed since my father's death; and it had also been two years since Carole had seen my father in a vision. Carole's fears about how *something was going to happen to Christopher in two years* had defiantly become a horrific reality.

Mike arrived to drive us to his home. Feeling somewhat bewildered and discouraged, we left the Reams Clinic. We were putting another part of our quest for a miracle behind us. To our surprise, Christopher seemed to be a little more responsive and feeling a bit better. We were to spend the night with Mike and Sandy and then make arrangements for Christopher's admission to Johns Hopkins Hospital the next morning.

As we traveled the interstate outside York, Pennsylvania, where we had lived before moving back to Georgia, Mike drew our attention to a Chucky Cheese Restaurant. Just a year before, we had celebrated Christopher's third birthday there. What happy memories they were! Who would have ever dreamed that now, on his fourth birthday, instead of eating cake and ice cream and having fun with friends and family, we would be fighting for his very life.

A True Emergency—Baltimore, Maryland, January 1985

Sandy was eagerly awaiting our arrival. She had prepared the guest bedroom for our overnight stay. We visited for a while and attempted to get liquids into Christopher before putting him to bed. We thought he had slept well that night. Then just before dawn, we were horrified to discover that he was not sleeping but was in a comatose state. We couldn't arouse him! A 911 call was immediately placed. The para-medic team arrived within minutes. After checking his vital signs, they gave Christopher oxygen, put him on a stretcher, and then wheeled him to the ambulance. In the dawning hours of that cold winter morning, with horns blowing, sirens screaming while weaving its way through traffic, the ambulance raced toward Johns Hopkins Hospital. Carole rode in the back with the paramedic as I sat up front with the driver. She watched in total shock as the monitor indicated that Christopher's vital signs were unsteady.

Carole repeatedly asked the paramedic, "How is he doing?"

He would answer the same each time, "Fine." But she knew our only child was near death. Here are Carole's words to describe the situation:

> I knew our son was near death. I knew that they were doing everything they could do to save his life. They tried to assure Neal and me that he was fine, but I knew in my heart that he was close to taking his last breath. I thought I didn't have much time left with him and my hope for a miracle was just about to run out. I tried to hold back my tears. I had to be strong. Somehow I thought Christopher could sense my presence and my feelings. I kept telling him how much I loved him and that he would always be the sunshine of my life.

The driver was in constant communication with the hospital. When we arrived, the paramedics quickly wheeled Christopher into the emergency unit. To our dismay, we had been directed to the wrong wing of the hospital. Tension mounted as the girl at the desk, nonchalantly chewing her gum, flipped through the admittance directory and said, "There is no Christopher Pylant on the books."

At this point, the irritated paramedic said, "Listen lady, we have a dying child out here! Now let's do something." She finally told us to take him to the children's wing at the other end of the hospital. The hospital was so large with the children's wing located about another city block away from where we were. Our son's life was hanging by a thread. We struggled to keep up with the paramedics as they rushed through the hallways, wheeling Christopher's gurney as fast as possible.

A young neuro-oncologist met us and immediately took Christopher in for an examination. Christopher was paralyzed, comatose, and hardly breathing. His blue eyes rolled uncontrollably in their sockets as the doctor moved his head from side to side. Barely alive, his body began to draw into the fetal position.

Carole, shaken and somewhat numbed from what she had just witnessed, returned to the desk for the normal admittance procedure. Mike had followed us there and stayed with Carole while I was with Christopher. It was hard for me not to give way to my emotions. I was very fatigued but had to remain calm and keep my mind alert and attentive. Christopher was taken directly for a CAT scan, which truly seemed to take forever.

Carole returned from admissions and together we sat in silence in a Johns Hopkins' waiting room, about to hear the results of the scan, our hearts filled with trepidation.

After what seemed like an eternity, Dr. Freedman, a renowned neurologist, came out to give us the news. He told Carole and me that the scan revealed a dark mass of tumors that had accumulated on the outer right side of the brain stem, causing extreme pressure on both the brain stem and the cerebellum. Although the main tumor could not be removed, the doctor stressed that to give Christopher some relief, the mass needed to be excised. However, his weakened condition made surgery impossible.

In the pediatric ICU, our child lay encased by wires and tubes connected everywhere to his small body. Machines monitored his every life function. Nutrients flowed into him intravenously. No food by mouth was permitted in case a sudden emergency required surgery. Christopher regained consciousness, but was unable to turn over, speak, or even swallow. His eyes, filled with desperation, sought to communicate to us his fears, pain, and insecurity. We felt the need to reassure and support him, so one or both of us stayed with him around the clock.

We continually spoke comforting, loving words, telling him and indirectly ourselves, "You will be okay. You will be well soon." The words sounded hollow as we desperately fought to purge any alarming emotions from our faces or voices.

The chilling atmosphere of death seeks to cut off hope—both for the moment and for the years to come. Christopher was the only male in our family line that could carry on the Pylant name. If he died, our generational legacy would be lost. A feeling of despair now gripped me as I stood there. Life itself was seeping from my son—all the promises of God seemed *no* and *never* in that moment, instead of *yes* and *amen* (see 1 Cor. 1:20).

Lost in memories and thoughts, I was startled back to reality as Christopher's team of young doctors slipped into our ICU room. They introduced themselves and began asking the same questions we had answered for our son's previous physicians. Heading the team was an African American pediatric neurosurgeon, Dr. Benjamin S. Carson. We tried to focus our exhausted and fear-filled minds to answer the dozens of questions bombarding us.

Carole and I clung to the bedrails, propping ourselves up—fatigued, worried, and about to collapse. If we had had an audio recorder we could have simply played a voice recording of all the myriad of answers we had supplied in the past to an endless chain of doctors, medical technicians, nurses, and nutritionists. We were nearing the end to our quest for a miracle to save our little boy's life. The efforts of the doctors, prior to reaching Johns Hopkins Hospital, fell hopeless to stop Christopher's plummet to death.

I couldn't help wondering if this young team of doctors had been assigned to Christopher's case just for a learning experience, as it had previously been determined hopeless. I tried to trust that God was in control. We struggled to cling to our tattered convictions for God to heal our son. This was the last team of experts. Our hope began to fade as Christopher's strength slipped away. The questions seemed endless, and our emotionless answers now came by rote as our subliminal doubts increasingly drowned our faith with a veil of fatal darkness. Death's icy fingers chilled that ICU room and slowly encircled our hearts.

Chapter 8

At War

Johns Hopkins Hospital—January 1985

Dr. Carson and his team exited from the ICU after concluding their meeting with us. Two other children were being treated in ICU along with Christopher. As we fought our thoughts of fear and battled the paralysis of not knowing what to do next, we talked with the mother whose daughter was also being treated by Dr. Carson.

She revealed that Dr. Carson was a Christian who prayed before each surgery. During all our previous hospital experiences, all our doctors did everything possible for Christopher physically, but spiritually we had been left to our own devices. When we discovered Dr. Carson was a Christian, we felt God's Spirit had not only sustained us to this point but had also guided us to the Johns Hopkins Hospital, placing Christopher into Dr. Carson's caring hands.

Once again, Carole and I spent all our waking hours at the hospital. We worked out a plan: I would sit with Christopher until about 1:00 a.m. while she rested in the children's playroom. We had pushed four armless chairs together into a makeshift bed. Carole's mother, Frances, and her younger sister Sandy ran laundry detail. They kept us supplied with a change of clothing we kept in a garment bag, which we placed under Christopher's bed.

Our love for Christopher motivated us beyond our physical limitations. We had never left Christopher's side from the beginning of his illness because we were determined to keep our family unit together and give each other the support that was so vitally needed.

Faith in God seemed to sustain us when our physical abilities began to wane. For some, the words *cancer* and *death* seem synonymous. We believed death wasn't an option. In the midst of our battle to save Christopher's life, we remembered that Jesus and life were equivalent. We meditated on the truth, *"The thief (Satan) does not come except to steal, and to kill, and to destroy. I (Jesus) have come that they may have life, and that they may have it more abundantly"* (John 10:10).

While Carole and I were desperately trying to cling to our faith and allow it to grow, Satan seemed to meet us at every turn, bringing doubt and bad reports, trying relentlessly to steal our hope, destroy our faith, and to ultimately kill Christopher.

The war raged: life versus death; faith versus doubt; God's promises and truth versus bad reports; light versus the valley of death's shadow.

The next shadow approached with its ominous, bad report.

At Death's Door

Dr. Carson returned to our room. He and his colleagues, along with the radiologists, had studied Christopher's brain scan. All concluded that he had a defused brain stem tumor. Since the tumor had attached itself to the brain stem, surgery was not an option. Dr. Carson's recommendation: "Take Christopher home and make him as comfortable as possible, for he will not live much longer."

"No, Dr. Carson," I emphatically proclaimed. "Our son will not die! I have faith that God will heal him." That earlier declaration engraved on my heart by the finger of God was uttered with every ounce of tenacious boldness within me.

All my previous conversations with Dr. Carson had led me to believe that his faith and his being a father of three had given him something more than medical realities to work with. Empathy and compassion filled his conversation. In this dire moment filled with hopelessness, I felt that the Holy Spirit was gently nudging him to try something more. I believed that God would work through him. In the midst of the darkness, a ray of hope shined. With much perseverance we continued to trust God for a miracle.

Dr. Carson finally conceded, "Okay, I'll take an MRI. Maybe this will show something different." When he came in to give us the report, sadness was apparent in his eyes. In his gentle, caring way, he said, "The MRI showed the same. Your son has a defused brain stem tumor." He added, "I'm sorry, there is nothing more I can do."

"But, Dr. Carson, we can't just give up! There's got to be more you can do," we responded.

"The most I can do is to go in and remove as much of the mass that has accumulated on the right side of the brain stem as possible," he responded. "This will give Christopher some temporary relief from the pressure on the brain stem and the cerebellum that has contributed to his paralysis. Then I will order a biopsy to determine the grade of the cancer and perhaps we can administer radiation treatments in hopes of extending Christopher's life."

Palliative treatment, but certainly no miracle was Dr. Carson's therapy. So after a week in ICU, Christopher gained enough strength to withstand major brain surgery. The surgery was scheduled to last more than six hours. A nurse took us into the ICU to prepare us for the gruesome sight we might encounter. We were told if Christopher survived the surgery, he would be placed in recovery with all sorts of tubes and wires on his body, which might include life-supporting devices.

Family members joined Carole and me in the waiting room for the six-hour wait. Carole and I remained strong in our faith. We prayed that when Dr. Carson opened Christopher's head, he would find the tumors had disappeared. To our surprise, in less than two hours, Carole saw Christopher being wheeled down the hallway. With great expectation of hearing good news, we rushed out into the hallway to meet Dr. Carson.

"I'm sorry," he reported, "I couldn't do more for your son. It was just as I expected. There were dark malignant tumors everywhere. I couldn't even see the brain stem, which evidently has been consumed by the cancer. Without the brain stem, Christopher has no real life. I'm afraid there is no hope."

"No!" I retorted. "Christopher will not die! Our hope is in the Lord! I still believe God will heal him." Carole broke away from all of us, tears streaming down her face, running to the elevator as her father, her sister Terry, and I raced to join her. Reaching the main floor, Carole continued to run down the halls. She remained totally unresponsive to my inquiries as to where she was going.

I finally realized where she was headed when I saw the chapel sign. We had prayed there many times before, but now everything was on the line. Carole frantically pushed the door open, rushed into the chapel, and lay face down on the floor before the altar, hysterically crying out, "God, if You won't heal Christopher, please let him die and be at rest! I can't bear to watch him suffer any longer!"

Exhausted and spent, I prayed next to her with hollow words. We both knew we had done all we could do. Now it was time to give our son back to God. When Carole finally calmed herself, we knelt side by side to lay Christopher (spiritually speaking) on the altar, a symbolic sacrifice before the Lord. We relinquished our hold on our precious child, releasing him back to his Creator, asking that His perfect will would be done.

Darkness fell. Shadows filled the room. Hope vanished. Night came for us, but not for our son.

THE UNEXPLAINABLE

The time came for us to visit Christopher in the ICU. As Carole and I entered the room, we held our breath expecting to see some sci-fi scene the nurse had described before he was taken into surgery. We were shocked, and very much relieved, to see our son lying there, sleeping very peacefully. The presence of his angels were felt in that room. There were only a few wires attached to his body for monitoring purposes and a little oxygen tube at his nose. Thankfully, there was no life-support machine necessary. I held his hand as Carole gently placed a kiss on his cheek and whispered very softly, "I love you, Christopher." His muscles were relaxed with no signs on his face of the distortion caused by the paralysis. We stood in silent prayer, thanking God for bringing him safely through the surgery.

Just before he was to be transferred from the ICU, a nurse came to say there was some concern that Christopher had been exposed to chickenpox. In his weakened condition, it could be fatal if he contracted the disease. Therefore, it would be necessary to place him in quarantine.

At this point, the tremendous strain on our mental and physical stamina was unraveling us. We prayed, "Lord, how much more do we have to endure? There seems to be nothing but discouragement at every turn. The satanic forces are persistent in their efforts to penetrate our souls; the enemy is using every weapon in his arsenal to defeat us. Please, dear Lord, renew our strength and give us favor and the tenacity needed for each new day. In the name of Jesus, we pray, Amen."

YOU CALL *THIS* BLESSED?

From the window in our hospital room, we watched people walking the sidewalks, many with young boys and girls at their sides. We wondered if they realized how blessed they were to have healthy children. It can become very easy to take life for granted. Now that our world had been turned upside down, we realized more than ever before how fragile it can be.

We took turns keeping a constant eye on Christopher. Regardless of how much medication he received, he lay sleepless for long periods of time. Due to the paralysis, there was no feeling in the left side of his face. He had chewed his bottom lip, causing it to swell and become ulcerated. He was also being fed through a feeding tube because of his inability to swallow. In order to keep moisture in his mouth, we swabbed it out with saline solution. And we turned him periodically to keep him from getting bedsores.

Although some of the tumors that caused pressure on his brain stem and cerebellum had been removed, much damage had already been done, affecting many parts of his body. The muscles in his legs began to tighten so severely that both his feet were drawn downward with his toes curling under. The nurses asked if we could massage his feet and legs and gently push his feet in the opposite direction to help keep the muscles stretched. It was becoming more and more unbearable to watch Christopher suffer.

Dr. Carson had given us the grim report after surgery. He didn't think Christopher could live much longer, yet we continued to see him lingering in a horrible, seemingly hopeless, condition. Carole reached a place where even the light of the sun became dark. As her husband, I couldn't even understand the condition of her heart; I was afraid for her health—emotionally, spiritually, and physically. Every time she looked out of the hospital room window, she felt imprisoned with no way out. She didn't know what *normal* was anymore and felt that her horrible nightmare would never end. Her heart would break each time she looked at her child—she was dying with him moment by moment.

The long and strenuous battle had taken a severe toll on Carole. Her emotions had been torn to the point of sheer desperation. While seated at a table, downstairs in the hospital's cafeteria, Carole revealed to me her plans of euthanasia and suicide if she didn't see a positive change in Christopher's condition soon. While she was alone with Christopher in his hospital room, she planned to use a pillow to smother him. Then she would take a couple of bed sheets from the maid's cart, parked in the hallway, tie them together, and then hang herself in the restroom.

LOSING MORE THAN A SON—JOHNS HOPKINS HOSPITAL—JANUARY 1985

Needless to say, I had been stunned to hear what Carole's deranged thoughts were at the deepest point of her distress. I told her, "Carole, I know how much you love Christopher. You feel life without him would be impossible. It's unbearable for both of us to see him suffer. But remember that we have given him back to God for His perfect will to be done. If Christopher is not to live, it will have to be the Lord's way and timing, not yours. When my life is over, I plan to be reunited with Christopher in heaven if he should not survive. If you commit murder, you might be separated from God and Christopher for all eternity."

We joined hands at the table and asked God to give us strength to carry on. It was sometime before I felt comfortable leaving Carole alone with Christopher. She finally came to the conclusion that there was no quick exit to get out of the deep, dark hole she was in. The road back was long and hard. I knew I had to protect Carole from her thoughts, encouraging her while fighting through my own fears and doubts. By encouraging one another, we soon noticed our moods and the atmosphere began to change. We slowly began to trust one another again, and God began to bring some light into our darkness.

As time passed, we realized the quarantine was a blessing in disguise. It gave us our needed privacy to pray and search the Scriptures while seeking the guidance and comfort of the Holy Spirit. We were in constant communication with Christopher, singing songs, reading to him, and reassuring him of our love, continually saying to him, "God is healing you. You will soon be doing all the things you loved to do."

We did not have our church family with us; and we did not have our biological families with us either. But we had each other! And we also had God's Spirit—the Comforter, the Counselor, and the Healer. His presence should have inspired great peace in us, but there was still this nagging "what if" that kept poking into our hearts.

All the staff knew of our belief that God was going to heal Christopher. Around 9:00 a.m. one morning, my mother called from Georgia. Carole was out of the room while a nurse, wearing her protective garb, came in to clean. Christopher was in my arms as I sat on the side of the bed attempting to hold the receiver in one hand and him with the other. Suddenly, he became upset and began to resist me. For fear he would pull out the feeding tube and dislodge the monitoring wires, I told my mother I couldn't continue our conversation. In total frustration, I tossed the receiver down onto a chair and cried out with a loud voice, "God, why have You forsaken us?"

The nurse abruptly turned to me and said, "What's wrong, Mr. Pylant? Have you lost your faith?"

I felt embarrassed, angry, and humiliated! I believe God placed her there at that very moment. It shocked me when she asked me that question. Realizing what I had said, I retorted, "No, I have not lost my faith!"

I was discovering that in the midst of fears, doubts, discouragements, and bad reports, our emotions can churn and roll like the ocean waves. Nonetheless, we are not capsized by emotions when we cling to the rock of God's truth. Christopher was our promised seed. God had clearly spoken that he would not die. The only ones who could cause us to capsize and sink the boat of our faith were Carole and me!

WORDS OF HOPE

The telephone rang almost immediately after placing the receiver on the hook. It was around four that afternoon. Jerry Joiner, from the River of Life Church, called, saying the prayer counsel at the River of Life Church felt they had a word from the Lord. He told us, "You have done all you can do. Now stand, for it is His battle."

We found those words in Second Chronicles 20:15, *"Do not be afraid or discouraged because of this vast army. For the battle is not yours, but God's"* (NIV). Jerry also said we should read Psalm 91, putting in Christopher's name where applicable. Carole and I began reading Psalm 91 from the King James Version to Christopher many times each day and night. Here is how we would pray for our child:

[Christopher] *that dwelleth in the secret place of the most High shall abide under the shadow of the Almighty.* [Christopher] *will say of the Lord, He is my refuge and my fortress: my God; in Him will* [Christopher] *trust.*

Surely He shall deliver [Christopher] *from the snare of the fowler, and from the noisome pestilence. He shall cover* [Christopher] *with His feathers, and under His wings shalt* [Christopher] *trust: His truth shall be* [Christopher's] *shield and buckler.* [Christopher] *shalt not be afraid for the terror by night; nor for the arrow that flieth by day; nor for the pestilence that walketh in darkness; nor for the destruction that wasteth at noon day.*

A thousand shall fall at [Christopher's] *side, and ten thousand at* [Christopher's] *right hand; but it shall not come nigh* [Christopher]. *Only with* [Christopher's] *eyes shalt* [Christopher] *behold and see the reward of the wicked.*

Because [Christopher] *hast made the Lord, which is* [Christopher's] *refuge, even the most High,* [Christopher's] *habitation; there shall no evil befall* [Christopher], *neither shall any plague come nigh* [Christopher's] *dwelling.*

For He shall give His angels charge over [Christopher], *to keep* [Christopher] *in all* [Christopher's] *ways. They shall bear* [Christopher] *up in their hands; lest* [Christopher] *dash* [Christopher's] *foot against a stone.* [Christopher] *shalt tread upon the lion and adder; the young lion and the dragon shalt* [Christopher] *trample under feet.*

Because [Christopher] *hath set his love upon* [God], *therefore will* [God] *deliver* [Christopher]: [God] *will set* [Christopher] *on high, because* [Christopher] *hath known* [God's] *name.*

[Christopher] *shall call upon* [God], *and* [God] *will deliver* [Christopher], [God] *will be with* [Christopher] *in trouble;* [God] *will deliver* [Christopher], *and honour* [Christopher]. *With long life will* [the Lord] *satisfy* [Christopher], *and shew* [Christopher] [His] *salvation* (Psalm 91 KJV).

One day, while still in quarantine, I mentioned to Carole how I missed the fellowship with our church family. God was always faithful to provide for our needs. Within two hours after saying that to Carole, a nurse stuck her head into the room. She said an elderly woman was asking permission to come in and pray for Christopher. I gave my consent.

In a few moments, a little gray-haired lady, dressed in a robe and a protective mask, appeared. She introduced herself as Rita Dondalski. She was the mother of Mary Ann Smidt, a co-worker of my sister-in-law, Terry Fishler. Terry had shared about Christopher's illness and the Lord had laid it on Rita's heart to come and pray for him. She explained that she was a member of the full gospel ministry and was Spirit-filled. She said for us not to be alarmed if we heard an unknown language and groaning sounds as she prayed; explaining that sometimes while interceding, these sounds rise up from deep within her.

Rita held Christopher close to her bosom. As she prayed, his countenance was brightened once again by the Holy

Spirit. Carole and I were thankful that God had sent Rita to pray for him. She gave us the encouragement we needed to continue our quest for a miracle.

On Monday, February 5, 1985, five days after surgery, Carole and I met with Dr. Carson, the young neuro-oncologist who initially examined Christopher, the radiologists, and selected staff members to discuss their final prognosis. The neuro-oncologist gave us the pathology report. He said the biopsy confirmed that Christopher was suffering from a grade four astrocytoma tumor with extensive necrosis. The prognosis was an estimated three months to live. We were told, since the mass had been removed, giving Christopher some relief from the pressure on his brain stem, we would see some brief improvement. However, the tumor would continue to grow very rapidly and eventually kill him.

Dr. Carson explained that the cancerous tumor would grow quickly in size, squeezing his brain stem, causing him to collapse into a coma and stop breathing. Radiation treatment was recommended with hopes of extending Christopher's life for a short period of time. Knowing the terrible affects radiation would have on his body, Carole and I agreed we would not have our son burned and tortured. We preferred that he have his life, no matter how short, without any unnecessary pain being inflicted. Therefore, we refused radiation treatment.

Having heard of our faith, the neuro-oncologist asked if we wanted to speak to a minister, a priest, or a rabbi. Carole responded, "I don't want to talk to anyone but God!" With Carole's answer to him, he leaned back in his chair, laughed loudly, and said, "I'm afraid He is not on our staff."

When I heard that statement, it was as if a sharp knife had plunged into my heart, its sharp blade stabbing and slashing, threatening to sever our last strains of hope. I really wanted to say to him, "Well, Doctor, perhaps you should consider hiring Him. You might save more lives," but I instead stayed silent. But regardless of all the negative reports that bombarded us, we maintained our trust in the Lord. He had given us strength to endure the battle to this point and we still had faith that He would carry us all the way to victory.

As if the devastating encounter we had just experienced wasn't enough, a confrontation with the radiologist soon occurred. He came to our room, apparently upset with our decision not to accept radiation treatments for Christopher. He inquired why we refused the treatments, saying, "Don't you want to help your son?"

After pressuring us to change our minds, Carole had had enough. She stood tall, looked straight into his eyes, and asked, "If you were dealing with the same circumstances, would *you* give radiation treatments to a member of *your* family?" There was no answer. He only abruptly turned and walked away.

The dark clouds of gloom and despair thickened and hung heavier than ever. A vital part of our lives was being taken away. The beautiful little boy that had given us so much joy and happiness was dying right before our very eyes. We would never again run and play with him on the beach, build sandcastles, or splash happily in the waves of the incoming tides. Never again would we take Christopher to the park and watch him feed the ducks as they swam on the lake. Never again would we see the excitement in those clear blue eyes as he opened his gifts on Christmas morning or on his birthday.

We were virtually empty and hopeless because our dreams were slipping away, being overcome by shadows of disease and death. Our hopes and expectations of Christopher maturing to become a fine, strong young man, finishing school and college, getting married and fathering children of his own, were quickly fading. The sand that sifted through the hourglass of Christopher's life was getting low. We were desperately trying to hold on to the thought that as long as there was breath in his body, there was still hope.

Carole and I were in constant prayer, hoping God would continue to hear the cries of our hearts: *"You, Lord, are forgiving and good, abounding in love to all who call to You. Hear my prayer, Lord; listen to my cry for mercy. When I am in distress, I call to You, because You answer me"* (Ps. 86:5-7 NIV).

Since Christopher was in ICU, we were unable to stay at the hospital. Carole's parents graciously made reservations for us at a hotel within walking distance to the hospital. It was so hard to leave him alone with strangers time and time again; so many surgeries, so many different faces and places surrounded him. The time away from him was unbearable. Every moment was precious and those moments were slipping away fast. We spent most of our hours at the hospital, which was comfort to us to know we were close to him, even though our visits were for brief moments in between. We felt the dark cloud hovering over us was becoming darker still.

Instead of hearing how he was going to live, we heard that he would live about three months and then he would die. *Death* was a hard word to say and it did not sit well in my vocabulary. Death was so final! Yet I know that dying gives some opportunity for hope.

Carole would speak to her mom many times and she would ask her about where we were going to bury Christopher if he died. Carole struggled with the thought within her and toiled with making any definite decisions. She could not bring herself to think of burying Christopher; therefore, she could not make or even think about making any decision at that time. Her parents had offered one of their twelve burial plots at the Jewish Har Sinai Cemetery in Baltimore County. It was a beautiful place, so serene and peaceful, situated on top of a hill under a tree.

We clung to a ray of hope that Christopher would not die; but the night rapidly approached and our tenacity for a healing was stretched to a breaking point.

Chapter 9

THE VALLEY OF SHADOWS

JOHNS HOPKINS HOSPITAL—FEBRUARY 1985

After receiving the last prognosis of an estimated three months for Christopher's life, Carole and I had to face the heart-wrenching fact that we might be burying our son. The time was rapidly approaching when we possibly would walk up to his coffin, saying our last good-byes to Christopher. Envisioning his little body, head shaved and scarred from so many surgeries, lying in a casket, was beyond our comprehension. As distraught as we were, we realized that preparations would have to be made for internment if he didn't survive.

Scripture reveals that when the storms of life come and the strong winds start to blow, our house (life) will not be destroyed if it is built on the rock, who is Jesus (see Matt. 7:24-27). I've concluded that the strongest house with its foundation built on the rock can be damaged but not necessarily destroyed. At the onset of Christopher's illness, we saw dark clouds beginning to gather and sensed that a storm was heading our way. With each devastating report concerning his condition, our storm increased in velocity. It soon turned into a hurricane with accompanying tornadoes. Now we found ourselves in raging turbulent waters of a catastrophic tsunami, crying out to God for rescue.

It's strange when we bring our burdens and lay them before the Lord, asking Him to take care of them, only to then pick them up again, struggling to carry them by ourselves. When Carole and I laid Christopher on the altar earlier, I hadn't left him there. Now I was desperately trying to trust God completely with my son's life. With a heavy heart, I made my way to the chapel and knelt before the altar. At that moment, I experienced the pain Abraham might have felt when he laid his *promised seed*, Isaac, on the altar.

I prayed, "Father God, I've come alone, in total surrender, to release my only son to You. I lay him on the altar, asking for Your perfect will to be done. If he is not to be healed, please take him to heaven and give him rest." Then, from deep within my spirit, words suddenly sprang forth. I heard my own voice declaring, "But God, I know You're not going to let Christopher die! I believe You have shown me in the book of Jeremiah that You have a purpose for his life!" That revelation was the "knot in the rope" that I needed. I held onto it tightly. Somehow I felt like my grip would keep that last thread from breaking.

When we have a promise from God, our part is to be faithful and hold on with tenacious perseverance to what God has revealed. Paul writes in Romans 5:1-5:

> *Therefore, having been justified by faith, we have peace with God through our Lord Jesus Christ, through whom also we have access by faith into this*

grace in which we stand, and rejoice in hope of the glory of God. And not only that, but we also glory in tribulations, knowing that tribulation produces perseverance; and perseverance, character; and character, hope. Now hope does not disappoint, because the love of God has been poured out in our hearts by the Holy Spirit who was given to us.

Carole and I lived out the truth of this process and promise from God.

1. We decided to have faith in Jesus Christ and enter into the grace of God. We had to trust Him—our own efforts and those of the medical professionals around us could not save Christopher.

2. With Christopher, we walked through the valleys, tribulations, trials, and sufferings. Carole and I agreed with God's promise for our seed to prevail generationally. Just as Abraham of old couldn't avoid his test and trial with Isaac, we could not avoid ours. Too often we seek relief from the tribulations instead of receiving from God's Spirit the strength, comfort, and endurance we need to stay the course, not quit, and finish the journey that Christ has put before us. He says to us, "Take up your cross and follow Me" (see Luke 9:23). No other way was open to us except the way of the cross—which just happens to be the way of suffering, pain, and dying to self.

3. Going through tribulation together developed in us perseverance—a tenacity to hold onto Christ, tightly grasp the power and comfort of the Holy Spirit, and unequivocally trust the promise of God. Did we waver at times? Yes. Did we feel like giving up at points in the journey? Yes. Did we quit? No! That's tenacious faith that is birthed out of the perseverance only God can shape in our lives. Why did we go through this? So we would develop *character*.

4. We are being conformed to the image of Christ (see Rom. 8:29). His character and likeness are being shaped within us so that His glory might shine through us. And His character, image, and likeness in us cannot be disappointed. Why? Because that is the true source of courage, strength, and hope given by the Holy Spirit.

OUR MIRACULOUS BREAKTHROUGH

Dr. Carson didn't expect Christopher to live. In fact, he fully expected him to continue to deteriorate and die in the hospital. Instead, Christopher progressively got better. His level of alertness improved. Both eyes started to focus and the difficulty with his bodily secretions improved. Dr. Carson couldn't understand why there was such a positive change in his condition. These changes prompted him to have another specimen of the tumor tested by pathology.

Something very strange was happening. Each time the reports came back, they were contradictory. Observing the sudden improvements in Christopher and considering the contradictory pathology reports, Dr. Carson ordered another CAT scan to be taken.

On Tuesday evening, Dr. Carson came in with the results of the scan. His face shone with excitement. With a tiny bit of tenacity in his own voice, he shared, "It looked as if the tumor had mysteriously pulled away from the brain stem, had turned, and popped free. The images from the scan showed that it was just sitting there not touching anything."

Carole began crying, laughing, and praising God all at the same time. Through her tears of joy, I heard her repeatedly cry out, "Thank You, Lord; thank You, Lord."

That was the ray of hope we needed. We read and reread these verses and continually repeated them to ourselves:

> *Yet this I call to mind and therefore I have hope: because of the Lord's great love we are not consumed, for His compassions never fail. They are new every morning; great is Your faithfulness. I say to myself, "The Lord is my portion; therefore I will wait for Him." The Lord is good to those whose hope is in Him, to the one who seeks Him* (Lamentations 3:21-25 NIV).

I questioned Dr. Carson, "You know who gets praise for this? God!"

He replied, "Yes, you're right Neal, for we doctors have been able to do little to help your son."

We remembered how Pastor Bob Wright and the elders at the River of Life Church had cursed the root of the tumor and commanded it to die in the name of Jesus. Carole and I gave thanks to God for honoring their prayers and our prayers. When we learned that the tumor had turned loose from the brain stem, that suggested the roots had died. Since the mass had been removed, it had room to pull away and pop free.

Dr. Carson told us it might be possible to go back in and clean out the remaining tumor, but it would be very dangerous. The tumor had now positioned itself behind large main arteries and blood vessels. If he were to clip one of them accidentally during surgery, it would be fatal. His suggestion was to release Christopher for a time of recuperation. He would then be readmitted for an arteriogram to determine the best way to proceed with surgery.

CHALLENGES AT HOME

That tiny flicker of hope was now a beacon! We again were fully convinced that Christopher would live. Our faith had taken a giant step forward and our tenacity had prevailed!

Though his condition improved during the next few days, it was still necessary for Christopher to be fed by a feeding tube. With staff assistance, Carole was instructed on how to insert the tubing through Christopher's nose. With her first attempt, the tubing came back through his mouth. I had a weak stomach for things like this and after observing that incident, I quickly rushed out of the room. I had to get away to get my emotions *and* stomach under control.

In reality, both Carole and I knew that neither of us would be able to accomplish such a grueling task. We prayed that he would be able to swallow and take food and drink by mouth before being discharged from the hospital. We worked diligently with the nurses to help Christopher regain his coordination so that he could handle liquids from a cup and eat soft foods from a spoon. Carole and I were relieved that he was able to consume enough nourishment without the use of the feeding tube just one day before his discharge.

Carole's parents were gracious to sacrifice their home and to move in with her sister Sandy and brother-in-law Mike during the two and a half weeks of Christopher's recuperation. They were always there with helping hands and giving hearts—their love was unconditional.

As head of the house, I had mixed thoughts and emotions as we pulled away from the hospital. I felt a great joy that God had answered our prayers and had brought us safely to this point. However, there were still many concerns about Christopher's frail condition and how we would manage during his recuperation time. Living day by day in the hospital was very stressful, but the trade-off was that we did have the assurance that our son was being cared for by medical professionals around the clock.

Realizing we would be home alone with a very sick child gave me an uneasy feeling. However, during all our previous experiences, we had learned to turn to God's Word for comfort and encouragement. Paul wrote to the Corinthians about his personal experience, *"But He* [God] *said to me, 'My grace is sufficient for you, for My power is made perfect in weakness.' Therefore I will boast all the more gladly about my weaknesses, so that Christ's power may rest on me. That is why, for Christ's sake, I delight in weaknesses, in insults, in hardships, in persecutions, in difficulties. For when I am weak, then I am strong"* (2 Cor. 12:9-10 NIV).

Christopher was soon able to handle a small amount of solid foods along with Sustecale, a nutritional liquid the dietitian had recommended. He had lost a good bit of weight. However, he surprised us all by quickly gaining five pounds as he grew stronger each day.

Arrangements were made for a physical therapist to come in twice a week to work with Christopher. Each day we assisted him with a regiment of exercises: rolling, stretching, holding him in a sitting position and shifting his weight from side to side, etc. How beautiful it was to see life returning to his little body; a body that had been weakened to the point of dying. We were encouraged to observe him displaying a great deal of inner strength with a strong determination to survive and to fully recover. In less than two weeks he was able to take my hand and pull himself up to a near sitting position.

Another growing concern was our finances. I had used part of the equity from the sale of our home and salon to purchase the assets of Kome Hair Design. All our income stopped when I walked away from the new business to take care of my family. The expenditures we had incurred with the rent of the apartment, car payments, and the new hair salon were quickly diminishing our monetary reserves.

While Carole was giving Christopher a bath, I went into the den and knelt before the couch, and prayed, "Lord, I feel I am where You want me to be, here to support Carole and Christopher. I cannot worry about our monetary needs right now. I'll turn all of these worries and concerns over to You. The Scripture says, *And my God shall supply all your need according to His riches in glory by Christ Jesus'* (Phil. 4:19)." Within days after I shared my concerns with the Lord, we received a check for $1,200. It was a love offering from the members of the River of Life Church. We thanked God for those wonderful people who were so generous in giving to meet the needs of their fellow Christians.

DIVINE VISITS

Mid-afternoon, the next day, I felt a need to escape for a while to try and clear the cobwebs from my head. We had stayed inside so long, keeping a watchful eye on Christopher, that the walls were beginning to feel like they were closing in on me. The weather was very pleasant for a winter day in Baltimore. There wasn't a cloud in the sky. The sun was shining brightly and there was just enough nip in the air to keep me alert. I left Christopher in Carole's competent care and just started walking.

The direction I walked took me past the tennis courts, clubhouse, and swimming pool, then down an old service road that was used when the condos were being built. It ran along the backside of a five-acre wooded track of land, which had been set aside by the developers for conservation purposes. A few feet to the right side of the road stood a large stone. It was so camouflaged by the shade cast from the canopy of a small grove of trees that I hardly noticed it. The stone reminded me of an artist's depiction of the one in the Garden of Gethsemane where Jesus knelt to pray. I tracked through the undergrowth that had covered the ground near the stone.

Once more, it was my hour to be alone with God, to contemplate the contents of my own "cup of sorrows." As I prayed, I said to the Lord, "Here I am, a man who stands a good chance of losing everything I've worked for. The life of my only son is hanging in the balance. The doctor tells me he could die if something goes wrong during the next brain surgery. Once again I ask You, O Lord, please don't let Christopher die!"

While sitting quietly amongst the beauty of nature surrounding me, I sensed His presence giving me a peace that surpassed my understanding (see Phil. 4:7). My weary soul was soothed and quieted by His assurance that He would never leave me nor forsake me (see Heb. 13:5). I returned with a new outlook! I had spent time in His presence and I felt revived and renewed.

That night, at bedtime, I was reading to Christopher from *My Jesus Pocketbook* publications. This particular story was about a short man named Zacchaeus. Jesus was walking down the road when a large crowd gathered to see Him. Because of Zacchaeus's height, he couldn't see what was happening. So he decided to climb to a high branch of a tree in order to have a better view. As Jesus came near the tree, He stopped and said, "Zacchaeus, come down because I'm coming to your house today" (see Luke 19:1-10).

At this point I stopped reading and said to Christopher, "Wouldn't it be nice if Jesus were to come to our house?" He nodded yes.

Then I asked him, "Has Jesus ever visited you?" Again he nodded yes.

"Where were you when Jesus visited you?" I asked.

I initially thought he told me, "In the room." Because of the paralysis, Christopher had lost the ability to speak clearly, making it difficult to understand him. His speech was as a baby's might be when learning to talk.

I began to guess which room. I asked, "The bedroom? The bathroom? The kitchen?"

Each time I would make a guess, Christopher would shake his head no. He finally reached over, picked up his mother's nightshirt and pointed to her stomach, and said, "Womb—in the womb." Carole and I were shocked. Our minds flashed back to the first time he had made a reference to the womb. How could a child that had never been taught of such things know where her womb was located?

I then asked Christopher, "Did Jesus talk to you?" Again, he nodded yes.

Naturally, my next question was, "What did Jesus do when He visited you?"

At that point, Christopher's face puckered as if he were going to cry. He then cradled his arms and rocked them from side to side, as a mother or father would cuddle a baby, indicating that Jesus held him in His arms.

We discovered later that passages in the Bible tell of God's dealing with the unborn child. The Living Bible reads in Psalm 139:15, *"You* (Lord) *were there while I was being formed in utter seclusion. You saw me before I was born and scheduled each day of my life before I began to breathe."* And in Jeremiah 1:5 we read, *"I knew you before you were formed within your mother's womb; before you were born I sanctified you and appointed you as My spokesman to the world"* (TLB).

Christopher always slept between Carole and me on the king-sized bed during his recuperation. Many times I would wait until he fell asleep, and then go to the living room sofa to sleep. During the wee hours of the morning, Christopher's movements awakened Carole. At that time, he was still unable to turn his body over by himself. Carole watched in amazement as he rolled to the edge of the bed. When she started to reach for him, he would suddenly roll back in the opposite direction. Then, as if unseen hands were playfully lifting and tossing Christopher, he began to laugh and giggle happily.

With all the startling things that occurred during that night, Carole asked him the following morning, "Christopher, did Jesus visit you again last night?" He nodded his head yes.

"What did Jesus do?" she asked.

With his little mouth perfectly formed, he said, "Shhh, it's a secret."

We could only look at him with amazement, believing God was dealing with him in a very special way.

AN UNUSUAL INCIDENT

Later that morning, around 9:00 a.m., after feeding Christopher breakfast, Carole left to visit her mother. She had been admitted to Johns Hopkins Hospital and was being treated for double pneumonia. I took Christopher into the living room to help him with some of his exercises that the physical therapist had assigned us. When we started the exercises, he said to me, "I'm tired."

"What do you mean you're tired? You've just gotten up," I jokingly shot back. What he said to me next caught me completely off guard.

"Dad, Adra is still in me." I immediately carried him to the bedroom and laid him on the bed. Again, he repeated, "Dad, Adra is still in me."

I asked him, "Who is telling you that Adra is still in you?"

"Grandmother."

This sounded very strange to me. Christopher didn't have a relative he referred to as Grandmother. He called Carole's mother "Nanny" and my mother "Mama."

Christopher, "Who is *Grandmother*?" I asked him.

He replied, "I don't know."

I was totally perplexed and wondered, Why would Christopher speak of a person he didn't know? And why would she tell him that this "Adra" was still in him?

When Carole returned from visiting her mother, I repeated to her what Christopher had said. She put him on her lap and also asked, "Who is telling you these things?"

"Grandmother told me that, and Papa sent me down to earth," he replied. He shared in such a matter-of-fact way that it seemed believable.

This was just such a bizarre story! We wondered if anyone would ever believe us. We flipped through our mental memory bank for someone we could share this with, someone who wouldn't think we were a couple of "loony tunes."

Unexpectedly, the doorbell rang in the middle of our dilemma. Rita Dondalski's daughter (the woman who came by to pray for Christopher at the hospital), Mary Ann Smidt, stopped by for a visit. After telling her all the strange things Christopher had said, she suggested I call her minister to get his thoughts on what was happening. Taking her suggestion, I called him and shared what Christopher had said, especially about his Papa sending him down to earth. His opinion was that our son may have had a near death experience and suggested that he had spiritually traveled and came back.

Wow! I thought. I had read a couple of books with stories of people having near death experiences. I have to admit they were interesting and very fascinating reads. At the same time, in the back of my mind, I couldn't help questioning their validity. If the minister's suspicions turned out to be true, then we had proof positive that this sort of thing does occur in life; or should I say, between life and death. Nevertheless, our main concern was Christopher's survival. We had to put all of this on the back burner and deal with it later.

Chapter 10

BACK TO THE HOSPITAL

Christopher was readmitted to Johns Hopkins Hospital on March 4, 1985. At that time Dr. Carson called us in for another roundtable discussion. We found ourselves once again on the same set, same table, same chairs, with the same players in attendance: the young neuro-oncologist, the radiologist, selected staff members, and of course, Dr. Ben Carson. Yes, we were still seated with the doctor who did not believe that God was on their staff. However, this time the smugness and mocking of God did not occur. The difference now was that the script had been rewritten.

Last time we had heard nothing short of a death sentence pronounced for our son. This time no one spoke except Dr. Carson. He said that he and his colleagues had studied the MRI that was taken before Christopher was released for recuperation. To their astonishment, they detected a tiny thread-like remnant of a brain stem. It had been pushed up into the cerebellum by the pressure from the mass that had been removed previously. During the first surgery it appeared that the cancer had completely consumed Christopher's brain stem.

With their *new* discovery it appeared that the tumor had not actually infiltrated the brain stem, but had adhered itself to it. Dr. Carson added that since the tumor had mysteriously pulled away, its new position had itself lodged *behind* vital arteries and blood vessels, making surgery feasible but very risky. An anterior gram was scheduled to be taken. The results would give the best and safest way to proceed with surgery.

Dr. Carson felt optimistic that the remaining tumor could be removed and Christopher would recover to live a long and healthy life. Perhaps the unusual things that were happening in Christopher's case would cause them to see these "religious fanatics"—as some had thought us to be—in a completely different light. Maybe they would realize that God was indeed on their staff after all.

The anterior gram was performed. Dr. Carson came in and excitedly exclaimed, "We're in *Fat City*! The tumor has moved completely away from any of the arteries and blood vessels that were presenting the problems." Our hearts exploded with happiness until he stopped us: "However," he said, "because of the tumor's new position, I will not be able to use the old incision as planned. To get to its new location, I will have to make a new midline incision."

My mind exploded with emotions! I was shocked, elated, and grateful. I probably felt a hundred emotions all at the same time—it took a few seconds for me to realize and comprehend what I was actually hearing. Of course I felt concern about a new incision, but my immediate reaction was to remind Dr. Carson, "God has answered our prayers and killed the root of the tumor."

We knew that God had performed a supernatural miracle when He visited Christopher during that special night while he was recuperating. Our old archenemy, Satan himself, wanted us to know he was still in the ball game. Although the score was now looking more favorably for the home team, we were not to home plate yet. We had just made it safely to third base. His harassing demons were always on hand to do their job.

When the time came to take Christopher to surgery, he was not sedated as he had been before with the other five operations. When the attendants came into the room to wheel Christopher to the OR, this time he became terribly frightened and wouldn't allow them to place him on the gurney. I told them I would carry him. When I picked him up, he began to resist with all his strength. The IV tubing was still in his arm. And when he swung at me, the stationery board struck my head, knocking the IV loose and causing the needle to pull out.

I said to Carole, "I don't think I can handle him."

She said, "Give him to me!"

With a calm and soothing voice she consoled him by saying, "Don't be frightened, honey. We are on our way to victory, and you're going to be all right."

SURRENDER ONCE MORE

Once again we felt the forces from hell rising up against us. It was a traumatic experience trying to constrain our son in order to get him to surgery. We finally reached the OR on the seventh floor. Christopher had calmed down enough to allow us to lay him on the gurney.

When the anesthesiologist came out to see what was going on, he saw the IV had been pulled out. He said with disgust, "What do I do now?" Christopher's veins in his arms, feet, and legs had been stuck so many times there didn't seem to be a good vein left to reinsert the IV needle. At this point they started to take Christopher in to be prepped. He began to resist again. I reminded them that the head anesthesiologist had promised to allow Christopher to be sedated while still with us. The attendant said he would check with the nurse.

Time crawled, but in a couple minutes the nurse came out to say, "The surgeons are ready for Christopher and you are holding everything up! You are not allowed to stay with him until he is sedated. Please leave."

I used every ounce of authority I could muster and told her, "You go back in there and tell them that if this is the case, there will be *no* surgery!"

She turned and stormed back into the OR. Reluctantly, they finally agreed to let me enter through the large double doors and hold our son in my arms until he was sleeping peacefully.

As I recall, Carole and I were waiting alone during this surgery. We had many who were supporting us in prayer, but we waited this one out, just the two of us. We spent time praising God for the days that lie ahead of us and for leading us through that deep, dark valley. It was such a hodge-podge of thoughts and feelings; kind of like being on a roller coaster where you couldn't see any scenery until you were right there staring at it. We had been on the ride of our lives, but it had not been anything close to a thrill ride! Was it possible that the little car that carried the three of us was finally coming into the station so we could get out?

It had been close to two hours when Dr. Carson came out to meet with us. Instead of the sad look of defeat we saw on his face after the previous surgery, he wore a big smile of victory. He said, "We were able to get it all! This time when I opened him up, I was amazed to see that the tumor had turned cystic and had become transparent enough to see through it. Where it had seemed so impossible to define planes before, I was suddenly able to lift the mass away in layers. After cleaning out all the crevices, there it laid, a healthy, gray brain stem, intact, but flattened and distorted."

Just as that tumor had filled in every crevice in Christopher's brain, hope and joy flooded into our hearts and filled us to overflowing. Dr. Carson shared in our victorious moment and we praised God together!

The surgery had been a great success. Word of our victory quickly spread. Nurses came in and asked if we would be willing to visit with other patients and their families to encourage them. We were able to share our walk of faith and how God had honored us, assuring them that the Lord was no respecter of persons (see Rom. 2:11), and He could do the same for them.

THE SURGEON'S REPORT

Many years later, Dr. Ben Carson wrote a book entitled *Think Big: Unleashing Your Potential or Excellence.* He took several pages to share his experiences (both professional and spiritual) about the faith journey that he took with us.

Christopher lay on a stretcher, scarcely breathing and barely moving. He was a pale, blonde child, almost a skeleton, with his eyes crossed. He looked so pitiful....

"Dr. Carson," Neal said, "we know that the Lord is going to heal our son. We came here to Johns Hopkins after much prayer. We felt that if we came here with our son, we would find a Christian neurosurgeon who could help Christopher. When we learned that you are a Christian, we knew we had come to the right place...."

Frankly, the parents' attitude took me aback. I had never before or since encountered parents who talked with such an obviously sincere conviction. Although I honestly couldn't give them a single bit of hope, I wanted to do something. Finally I said, "Here's what I'll do. I'll at least show the X-rays to the radiologists. Maybe they can see something that I don't."

...After closing things up, I went immediately to the Pylants, I felt both sad and uncomfortable. I repeated what some would call the usual platitudes. Mainly I just did not know what else to say. They had been so sure that I could remove the tumor.

After explaining what I had found, I said, "Look, I don't know why your son has this horrible malignancy. It can't be removed. Perhaps your son has already served his purpose in life. Only God knows the beginning and the end. Maybe you shouldn't question the reason for these things."

"Thank you, Dr. Carson, I know you're sincere," Neal said, "but the Lord is going to heal our son. I just know it."

"Your faith is admirable," I said, hardly believing that they could still declare so staunchly that God was going to heal their son. Not one flicker of doubt clouded their faces.

…I fully expected that Christopher would continue to deteriorate and probably die in the hospital.

Instead, Christopher got better—and no one was more surprised than I. His level of alertness improved, both eyes started to focus in the same direction, the difficulty with secretions disappeared. He moved more on his bed.

"What's going on here?" I asked myself…. "Let's get another CAT scan and a MRI." I could still see a large amount of the horrible tumor in the area of the brain stem. As I inspected more closely, however, I saw a small ribbon tissue in one of the corners. Is it possible, I wondered, that the brain stem was up there? Can it be that the tumor is outside the brain stem? That it's crushing and pushing the brain stem up there?

"We'd better go back in," I told the parents.

"Praise the Lord," Neal said so quietly that I had to strain to hear the words.

Carole's eyes filled with tears. "Oh, thank you, thank you," she said.

Back to the operating room, buoyed by the confidence that there was a ribbon of brain stem, I started sucking away tumor tissue. I found pockets and pockets of the mass. It had insinuated itself into every possible crevice and crack. Eventually I saw the ribbon of brain stem.

"There it is!" I said aloud. To my delight, I discovered that it really was the brain stem I had seen, and it was intact. It had become almost flattened, but once I removed the tumor it filled in the area. As I continued to work, I could hardly believe what I had discovered.

Over the next five weeks, the boy continued to get better....

Months later, one of the doctors who was working as a neuro-oncologist told me, "You may not understand what's happened to me, Ben. You see, I've been an atheist for a long time. Or maybe I just did not see any need for God. But the Christopher Pylant incident has changed my thinking. The faith of those people and the results in that boy, have had a profound effect on me." His words touched me just as much as his being honest enough to admit it. "I do understand the profound effect," I said.

"There's got to be something to religion," he said. "In fact, more than this, honestly, that has made me a believer."[1]

COULD WE JUST GET BACK TO *NORMAL*?

The next step was more physical therapy to help Christopher get on the road to recovery. Arrangements were made for a daily 30-minute session starting around 11:30 each morning. The therapist worked beautifully with Christopher, always encouraging him, saying, "Good job" when he accomplished a new or difficult task. Christopher always had such a positive spirit. He faced each obstacle with a smile and an I-can-do-it attitude.

Carole and I watched with tears of joy and mixed emotions as Christopher struggled to reclaim the things that had been stolen from him. The debilitating effects from the paralysis on his left side severely constricted and tightened his leg muscles. When he first tried to stand, he could only stand on his tiptoes. His foot would not lay flat on the floor, making it more difficult for him to walk. Leaned against a walker, he could barely hold on with his weakened hands but he still tried to put one foot in front of the other. He had difficulty lifting a lightweight beach ball over his head. What had once been so easy was now a struggle.

Crawling through a large circular hoop held by the therapist was a monumental task because of the weakness and lack of muscle coordination in his body. Due to the tremendous pressure on his brain and perhaps damage done to nerves during surgery, Christopher was rendered almost blind in his left eye and deaf in his left ear. Carole and I knew it would be a long time before seeing Christopher's full recovery. But with diligence and hard work, we had no doubt he would be able to enjoy his life again. Never again would we take for granted the natural abilities God had given us.

The day of Christopher's release from the hospital, Dr. Carson came in to say good-bye. He had such a kind and gentle nature, an aura of peace seemed to always surround him. He sat on the side of the bed and held Christopher on his lap. As their eyes met, I felt the love of God connecting them. A bond was established between Christopher and Dr. Carson that would last a lifetime.

Later, Christopher would share with us about his recollections of Dr. Carson:

> The very first recollection I have of Dr. Carson was the day I was leaving the hospital. On that morning, I remember a man walked into my room; he wore blue scrubs and a white lab coat and sat on my bed. Then he picked me up and placed me on his lap. He told my mom and dad, "Everything looks good. He is ready to go home." Then he looked down at me and smiled: our eyes met and I felt a deep connection that would stand the test of time. I knew he had done something special to help make me well.

Carole, Christopher, and I returned to her parents' condo to prepare for our trip to our home in Georgia. Carole and I knew the difficult tasks that lie ahead but we were determined to nourish and strengthen Christopher's body back to health. While we were excited to return home, Carole was very concerned about her mother. She was now in her own hospital room at Johns Hopkins Hospital with a tube inserted in her side to drain the mucus and blood from her lungs due to pneumonia. Not only was she suffering from her own pain but ours as well. Carole's heart cried in prayer, praying that Jesus Christ would reveal Himself to her and touch her sick body.

Carole's dad was very comforting, assuring her that her mother would be okay. He said the doctors told him that the road to recovery would take some time but eventually she would be fine. It was difficult for Carole to leave her family but she felt God's hand working in what she could not see.

Many years later, in January 2003, Carole's mother was diagnosed with stage four lung cancer. Carole was fortunate to have had some quality time with her before she died in April 2003. Her prayer for salvation for her mother was also answered. While Carole sat beside her mother's bed, reading Scripture from Romans 10:9-10: *"That if you confess with your mouth, "Jesus is Lord," and believe in your heart that God raised Him from the dead, you will be saved. For it is with your heart that you believe and are justified, and it is with mouth that you confess and are saved"* (NIV), she accepted the Messiah, Yeshua, Jesus as her Lord and Savior.

ENDNOTE

1.   Ben Carson, M.D., *Think Big: Unleashing Your Potential for Excellence* (Grand Rapids: Zondervan, 1992), 111-119.

Chapter 11

BACK HOME AGAIN

We arrived home on March 23, 1985—Christopher's Mama, Aunt Nene, and his sister Heather met us at the Atlanta airport. They had prepared a little welcome home surprise for him. There was a cake decorated with his favorite cartoon characters, Bert and Ernie.

It was so good to be back in our familiar surroundings again and sleep in our own bed. We had been broken and shattered. We had gone through the fiery furnace, having our faith tested to its max. We had faced evil as we walked through the valley of the shadow of death. Our greatest reward was gaining victory for Christopher's life and witnessing the defeat of our enemy.

Totally settling in took some time, especially for Carole. She recognized the importance in continuing a nutritional diet for Christopher. So Joyce Knapton was there for us once more. She ran a biochemical analysis for Christopher to determine his nutritional deficiencies. And soon Christopher started to show improvement in his overall health.

Then, to our surprise, he began speaking strange things again. I remember a friend of mine, who is an author, saying to us that when she read my manuscript, that she began to detect a prophetic layer beginning to surface. Her statement gave me more reason to consider that Christopher was speaking prophetically; that God had indeed put His words in his mouth. When I shared what Christopher was saying with the pastor, elders, or church members, many times they would try to give me confirmation through Scripture.

Christopher said he saw Satan being thrown into the flames of hell. He said, "I saw Jesus take blood from His stomach and throw it at Satan."

He told us of a visitation he had with Jesus in the living room of our home. So I asked him, "Did Jesus talk to you?"

Christopher smiled and responded, "Yes! Jesus told me, 'I AM, saith the Lord.'"

"Son, did Jesus say anything more to you?" I prodded.

He shook his head and said, "No, He just went up," pointing his index finger to the ceiling of the room.

While sitting at his play table, Christopher suddenly said, "I saw Papa in heaven. When Papa saw me he was very surprised. He told me, 'Christopher, you have to go back to your parents.'"

This encounter Christopher was describing strengthened my belief that God had taken my father on January 23rd, at 9:05 p.m.—the exact time and date of Christopher's birth two years earlier.

Other visions Christopher described caused me to believe also that my father was taken to be some sort of spiritual friend for Christopher while he lingered near death. His encounter with his Papa while in heaven explained why he had said his grandparent sent him down to earth and back to his parents.

Christopher would deliver Scripture from the Bible that I had never heard. It had to be the anointing of the Holy Spirit giving him knowledge of these things. We had taken him to church only twice when he was a baby and to the Jewish temple twice during High Holy Days. Otherwise, he had no exposure to any type of religious teaching.

ADRA RETURNS—LILBURN, GEORGIA, MARCH 1985

After returning home from Baltimore, we always read Scripture and said our prayers before going to sleep. One night, out of the blue, Christopher said, "Satan was a bear named Adra. Satan and God were fighting when I was in the womb."

I admonished him, saying, "Now stop telling these stories. I think you're just making them up when you talk about animals."

He didn't say anything more that night. But then, the very next night, he began saying the same thing. But this time he said, "Daddy and Satan were fighting when he was in the womb." Irritated that he was persisting with this and a little skeptical, again I stopped him and told him not to tell things that were not true.

A few days passed. He and I were sitting on the bed, talking and laughing. We loved those father and son times together. Then, unrelated to our current conversation, he again said, "Satan was a bear named Adra. Satan and God were fighting when I was in the womb."

This time I began to listen. I questioned him, "Christopher, you're always talking about a battle, where were you during this battle?"

He said, "I was pounding and pounding on nails." He made a motion with his clinched fist. "And with my screwdriver," again, making a motion with his hand.

I asked him, "What were you building, honey?"

With the total honesty of a child, he replied, "I was building a cross. Adra (the bear) was after me, and I hid behind the cross."

Then I asked, "Where was God during this battle?"

"God was in front of me and in the back of me."

This was such an extraordinary story, and he was so persistent to have me listen to him. I couldn't bring myself to believe this really happened—that he actually saw this vision. But yet, at the same time, I asked myself, *How could such a young child make up such a detailed and bizarre story?*

A few days later Patsy Joiner came into the salon. I shared what Christopher had said. She related that just recently she had been in prayer for our pastor. The Lord had given her three visions. Each vision revealed the pastor doing battle with a bear, which, as in Christopher's visions, the bear was symbolic of Satan. And in her third vision, the bear was defeated.

She said, "Now I think I understand why Christopher said he wondered what your name was when he was in the womb. As strange as it might sound, perhaps God was showing Christopher things that would take place in the future. While you were doing spiritual battle through prayer for his life, God placed you on the front line of battle with this bear (Adra/Satan). During these battles, Christopher experienced the Spirit of God all around him, as a shell of protection from the enemy, as he was hiding behind the cross."

A friend of mine had studied many types of religions, including Satanism. I shared Christopher's visions with him as well. His response was astonishing. He explained, "During satanic rituals, witches and warlocks call forth spirits from the darkness. These demonic spirits many times take on physical animal forms. The only one that comes as a bear is Satan himself." This being true, it gave validity to what Christopher had experienced when he said, "Satan was a bear named Adra, and Satan and God were fighting when I was in the womb."

One night, just before putting Christopher to bed, he began telling Carole and me that he had been with Jesus in heaven. So I asked him what Jesus was wearing.

He said, "Around His neck and down to the floor."

"You mean, Jesus was wearing a robe?" I asked.

"Yes, a robe," he replied.

"Was anyone else there with you and Jesus?"

"Yes, Papa was there."

"What was Papa wearing?" I inquired

"He was wearing a robe too, but Papa had on a hat."

"What color was Papa's robe?"

"It was blue and purple," he said.

"Was anyone else there?" I further inquired.

"Yes, Satan was there. He was wearing something around his arm so he wouldn't get hurt in the battle."

"Did you see anyone else?"

"Yes, Grandmother was there. Satan was fighting with Jesus and Grandmother was fighting with Papa."

Amidst our confusion, fascination, and doubt, we were hearing our son telling a story that was totally mind-boggling and beyond our comprehension. After Carole had taken Christopher to bed, I opened my Bible to read passages found in the Old Testament. That night I read from Exodus 28, which gave a description of the garments that were to be made for Aaron, the High Priest. What got my attention were the colors of his robe, blue and purple, along with others, just as Christopher had described in his vision. The High Priest wore a turban on his head as well. Christopher had said his Papa was wearing a hat. My heart suddenly skipped a beat when I realized what I was reading.

Needless to say, Carole got no more sleep. I questioned her, "Do you recall what Christopher told us before he went to bed?"

With sleep in her voice (and a little irritation), she shot questions back at me: "What do you mean? Why are you so excited?"

I showed her the Scriptures and pointed out that Aaron's robe was blue and purple and that he wore a turban, a type of hat. I said, "Christopher just told us that Papa was wearing a robe of blue and purple and was wearing a hat."

Carole looked confused, and asked, "So, what's your point?"

I exclaimed, "Carole, my father's name was Aaron!"

I thought through Christopher's encounter that God was revealing what I had suspected for a long time, a curse might have been put on the males of my family. I remembered that a "grandmother" told Christopher that Adra was still in him. Now, it was apparent that this "grandmother" in Christopher's vision had an alliance with Satan.

I thought perhaps, with regard to his Papa and Jesus, God was showing Christopher a parallel between the Old Testament and the New Testament. My father was appearing as the Old Testament High Priest, acting as a mediator for his grandson. And Jesus was appearing, as He is now, our High Priest of the new covenant, battling Satan for Christopher's life.

Many times while we were reading the Bible, Christopher would say, "Read Acts." He had heard of the book of Acts when we read to him earlier from *My Jesus Pocketbook ABC's* stories. But we wondered why he always insisted we read from the book of Acts. This mystery was about to be revealed in a mighty way!

ALL KINDS OF FOLLOW-UPS— BALTIMORE, MARYLAND, AUGUST 1985

In August 1985 we returned to Baltimore for Christopher's follow-up examinations at Johns Hopkins Hospital. Christopher was wearing white pants, a dress shirt, red suspenders, and a little bow tie. When we exited the plane and walked out to meet Carole's family, his radiant smile of victory lit up the whole terminal. The neuro-oncologist, who had stated during our roundtable discussion that God was not on their staff, was again the first to examine Christopher. To our surprise, he turned to me and said, "Mr. Pylant, you understand that man could not do anything to save your son's life. You have to thank the Man (God) upstairs."

Because of the damage to Christopher's left eye, he was scheduled to see an optometrist who, after giving his opinion, referred him to a doctor in Georgia. After seeing Dr. Carson and receiving the examinations report, we joined Carole's family for some downtime before returning to our home.

Arriving at Sandy and Mike's house, I went directly to the telephone and placed a call to Mary Ann Smidt. When she heard my voice, she said, "Neal, before you say anything, I have something to tell you. Two weeks ago I was reading in the book of Acts. This name *Adra* your son alluded to as a bear (Satan) literally jumped off the page at me. It's in Acts 27:2. Although it was used as a prefix to the name of a ship, I later ran reference in my main concordance and found the name of a demon (pagan god) with the same prefix. I've wondered if this could be the demon your son spoke of when he said 'the germ in my body that is making me sick is named Adra.' The reference says, *'The Avvites worshiped their gods Nibhaz and Tartak. And the people from Sepharvaim even burned their own children as sacrifices to their gods Adrammelech and Anammelech'* (2 Kings 17:31 NLT)."

I don't think she took a breath in the delivery of this message. You see, Christopher had insisted that Carole and I read from the book of Acts to him before going to bed each night. Now, Mary Ann was able to shed some light on this mystery and things were beginning to make more sense.

All those spiritual encounters we had once put on the back burner now took the forefront. Christopher had spoken so many extraordinary things Carole and I couldn't help but wonder if our child had a gift for storytelling coupled with a great imagination. There had been times I would reprimand him thinking he was making up untrue stories. It was not until I considered that God might be giving us confirmation to what Christopher had said in His written Word through the testimony of others and through unexpected venues that I began to listen with an open mind. Now, more from Christopher was about to come.

Christopher and I were sharing some time together, playing with some of his toys. He suddenly turned to me and said, "I saw Jesus in heaven."

"Where was He when you saw Him?" I asked.

"He was standing in a mist." He made a motion with his fingers, as describing falling rain.

"When Jesus saw me, He stepped out of the mist, took my hand, and said, 'Come with Me, Christopher, I want to introduce you to My Father.'"

It was some time after Christopher told me about seeing Jesus in heaven that I visited a friend who had a Christian band. While listening as they practiced their music, my heart leapt with surprise. There, at the base of the drummer's platform, was a picture of Jesus standing in the mist, just as Christopher had described. I knew in my heart that God was confirming what Christopher had experienced.

A vision was revealed to Cathy Stillwell, a member of River of Life Church, the morning we brought Christopher in for prayer. She saw him as an older child playing baseball, while Jesus assisted him. What Cathy saw in that vision was also confirmed in a picture found in a Christian bookstore—a young boy at bat with an image of Jesus standing behind him assisting him. Christopher's desire to play baseball came to pass when he played on a little league team. I don't believe these to be mere coincidences. I was not seeking confirmation on any of these things. Nonetheless, God can use whatever He chooses to speak to us.

Another picture, that was found when Carole and Christopher were shopping in a Christian bookstore, corresponded to a powerful vision Sheri Vultaggio was given during the service that same morning. The picture is of Jesus, sitting, with a group of young children surrounding Him, as He held a little boy's face that looked exactly like Christopher before his illness. Christopher said to his mother, "Look Mom, that's what Jesus did to me!"

The following is a copy of a letter Sheri wrote to Christopher in 1987.

Dear Christopher,

This is for you:

I remember a couple years ago (it seems longer to me now) that I was in Sunday school class—Joe and I were teachers—and Bill and Patsy Cochran asked for special prayer for a couple coming to church with their son who was diagnosed with a brain tumor and not expected to live. When I hear things like this about children, I always hurt down deep inside, and it disturbed me greatly to hear it, especially the fact the little boy was so young. We prayed in class for the parents to have an open heart to receive from the Lord.

We went to church and I, at that time, sat in the middle section on the aisle in the front pew. I sat there and we did our praise and worship part of the service. Then we sat down and were either still in a state of worship or praying. I can't remember exact details, but I do remember that in a very brief and quiet moment that I saw Jesus walking the aisles—not so much a solid form, but a presence with shape. He started way to the left of me and slowly walked down the left aisle and across the front and went on up the aisle next to me. He stopped at a couple sitting on the aisle—the man holding a child was sitting on the aisle. Jesus never said anything, but reached out and took the little boy's face in both of His hands. I don't remember words, but at that moment I knew that He had touched the child with His healing hands and that the child was healed.

At this time, I still did not know who the child was. We went on with our service, and at the end, Pastor Bob called the couple forward that had come for prayer with the little boy with the brain tumor. My heart skipped a beat when I saw who they were. I had been touched by my experience and hardly was aware of what went on the rest of the service until this moment and, as we prayed, I cried a lot because I just knew what Jesus had done.

I remember asking God to please give this couple His peace and love to be strong and courageous throughout what lay ahead. I also remember sitting and staring at the little boy, thinking how really bad he looked and having to finally close my eyes because my mind told me he wouldn't make it, because he looked so near death at that moment. But I closed my eyes and remembered Jesus's touch.

In fact, I hung onto that for a long time until the child was finally totally healed.

After church I really knew in my heart that I had to tell someone and I fought the urge to tell the parents. They didn't know me from Adam's house cat and I could well imagine how the words might sound to someone having to live with this very ill child day in and day out and have a woman come up and say, "I saw Jesus touch your little boy, and he is healed!" So, with heart in mouth, I went over to Patsy and told her and kind of left it at that.

It's special to me to be sitting here writing this to you, because you are healed and beyond that, being used by the very One who healed you. Every time I see you, and I do mean every time, I consider it a privilege to know you and watch you grow daily. You remind me continually of God's love and His grace and mercy.

Thank you, Christopher.

Love,

Sheri Vultaggio

Chapter 12

THE PERFECT ENDING

ALPHARETTA, GEORGIA, NOVEMBER 1985

While the medical follow-up was better than anyone could have ever imagined, all those things we had once put on the back burner to get Christopher's physical health back in order now took the forefront. We were concerned about his spiritual health as well as his physical—and ours too!

One evening, at a Christian group gathering, I shared how God dealt with Carole, Christopher, and me in supernatural ways. I shared Christopher's story about a germ named Adra and how I believed it was a demonic spirit. A gentleman, whom I'd never met before, asked if I knew a deliverance minister named Rev. Tom Hodgin. Within a span of 24 hours, another stranger asked me the same question. He gave me Rev. Hodgin's phone number. I could only believe that God had sent his messengers to direct my path to Rev. Tom Hodgin.

Deliverance may be an unfamiliar term for you. When Jesus walked the hills of Judea and Galilee during His early ministry, He declared that one purpose of His ministry was to "set the captives free" (see Luke 4:18-19). Often, when Jesus confronted a demonic spirit, He would "deliver" that person with a simple command like, "Come out of him." The early church knew that at the name of Jesus, demons would flee. And Christians through the ages have used the name of Jesus to deliver oppressed people who were in bondage.

So I wasted no time in picking up the phone and dialing the number of the pastor who was familiar with deliverance. Explaining the purpose of my call and relating to him all we had experienced, Rev. Hodgin suggested that before bringing Christopher, I should come for deliverance myself. He said that I would need to be cleaned and strengthened to face what might lie in the future while raising Christopher.

After my deliverance, Carole and I took Christopher to meet with Rev. Hodgin. It was November 1985. We sat and observed as Rev. Hodgin prayed and delivered Christopher of the demonic spirit named Adra.

We were astounded to hear what Rev. Hodgin saw in the spirit while he prayed. He said, "I saw a huge demon sitting on a throne, looking down, as if he was a ruler. His hands were resting on the arms of his throne, as you see President Lincoln's hands at the memorial in Washington, DC. When I bound him, in the name of Jesus, I saw large chains wrap his body, fastening him to his throne. When I cast him out, four imps came into the throne room. The throne collapsed, as if it were on hinges. The four little demons took the legion out, still bound by chains to his throne."

Adra had finally been brought down! Once again, God had opened Christopher's eyes to the spirit realm. When Rev. Hodgin had finished the deliverance, Christopher exclaimed,

"I saw Adra leave, he went that way," pointing upward with his index finger.

After his deliverance, Christopher's recovery seemed to be more rapid. He grew stronger day by day. Our hearts were joyful with the deepest, most inexpressible joy!

GROWING UP YEARS—LILBURN AND NORCROSS, GEORGIA, 1985-1999

Though he was still physically impaired, he was able to resume some of his normal activities. He attended K4 and K5 located at Killian Hill Christian School in Lilburn, Georgia. Although still struggling to recover from weakness, he was able to graduate with his classmates.

Because of the difficulty he had keeping up with the other kids and considering the severity of his illness, his K5 teacher was concerned that Christopher might have a learning disability. She suggested he be evaluated before enrolling him into first grade. The results of the evaluation confirmed Christopher did not have a learning disability. In fact, it was quite the opposite. God had performed another miracle, blessing him with a gifted mind and an IQ of 137. He entered grade school on schedule.

Being touched by Christopher and witnessing his life being restored, Joyce Knapton wrote this beautiful poem that follows:

Little child could it be you I see this very day?
Your eyes are straight; they once were crossed
You were too weak to play.
Little child, is it you who walks so tall and fast?
Daddy held you in his arms when I saw you last.

Who is this one who says a Psalm
with feeling and with ease?
Why it's Christopher renewed and
strong and down on his knees.
To thank You, Father, for his life,
to thank You for Your love.
Your will's been done upon this
earth, the same as it is above.

– JOYCE KNAPTON (December 29, 1987)

MY LIFE AT A GLANCE BY CHRISTOPHER PYLANT

Being smart was one thing, but there were some other challenges to deal with. I had to learn to read and write. Reading was not as much of a problem as writing. I struggled with math also. Physical education was a nightmare due to my unsteady balance. There were two exercises that were nearly impossible for me to do. One was a seesaw type board that I had to balance on, and the other was climbing a rope that hung from the ceiling. Being that they were aware of my physical limitations, the PE coaches encouraged me to do my best at whatever activity was scheduled for that day.

In second grade, the toughest part for me was math and learning cursive writing. I had a good personality and was able to make some friends. I had my first experience with music in second grade and I absolutely loved it. PE was still a challenge, however, but I remember Field Day was the first time I tapped into my inner strength and was determined to participate in what my peers were doing. Although I finished last in everything, I persevered and completed every single event.

Third grade was a pivotal year for me. I knew that I was different from the other kids. That was the year the mockers sowed their seeds of doubt into my life. By God's grace and supernatural tenacity, I was able to keep those voices at a quiet level and did not succumb to the fear of failing. A love of history was birthed in me that year as well. My third grade teacher did not feel I was ready to move on to fourth grade, but to the shock of everyone, I passed the scholastic exam and entered the fourth grade that fall. By the fifth grade, I was starting to accept myself and deal with my limitations.

In middle school, the reality of my limitations hit me full force. They were a major contributor to my feelings of inadequacy and loneliness. There was also the fact that I wore glasses and had braces.

The monster of peer pressure raised its ugly head and tried to devour another helpless victim. I was an object for teasing and an easy target for the bullies. They only could see my outer appearance, and because I was different, they decided to be mean to me, threatening to beat me up and leave me stranded where no one would ever find me. Their words were like poison arrows that just kept hitting my heart day after day. My dignity and self-esteem were stripped from me little by little. I began to give in to the pressure and started to believe the demeaning things they were saying about me. This challenge would take both mental and physical strain to defeat.

I would quote Bible verses to give myself encouragement, but I only did it in the secret place of my heart when I was in distress and alone. If it were not for God giving me strength and remembering His will for my life, I probably would not be here today.

After those numerous experiences, I began to observe people and was more cautious about who I talked with. Due to this peer pressure, I began to isolate myself from others and retreat into my shell. I separated myself from people unless I felt comfortable around them.

Finally something came along to boost my confidence. While still in middle school, I became interested in playing little league baseball. Due to having fair eye-hand coordination, I was not the best player on the team but was an encouragement to the other players, providing a good example of sportsmanship that helped us win trophies.

In high school, I enjoyed both music and drama. I was involved in chorus, show choir, theatre productions, and sang a solo in the high school talent show. Academically, I managed to maintain a 3.8 GPA and was awarded a Hope Grant at graduation.

I had written a few poems during the past years and was excited to have an opportunity to read a few publicly. I felt honored to have two of them published—"Time" and "Seize the Day." The poem that follows, entitled "My Prison," is mainly a reflection of my struggles in middle school.

"MY PRISON"
by Christopher O'Neal Pylant

I stand alone in the four corners
of a cold prison cell.
Fear is my ball and inferiority is my chain.

The only light is from a glass window.
I look out the glass window to the world outside.
Everyone seems so happy and free,
while I'm here confined in darkness
to be tortured by preconcep-
tions and opinions of myself.
Who am I? Where do I fit in this happy world?
I try to bang on the window for
someone to let me out
but no one heard.
I tried to scream, but an unseen
force restrains my speech.
Is this a dream?
Surely someone must have seen
me peer out the window.
No. No one can see me.
I feel like I am in an observation room
in which I watch them, but they
don't know I'm there.
Oh, the demons oppressing my brain
convincing me to think that I
am less than what I am.
I feel like I am drifting out on the
sea and no one even cares.
No lifeline, no lifeboat.
Just me and all my assumptions.
I wear masks to hide my true feelings.
So no one can see the darkness that lies within me.
I am invisible, I am insufficient
in a world of fakeness and facade.
No one sees the real me.
So, I am here in this prison cell

to be tortured and chained
to my preconceptions and opinions
until someone notices the real me and lets me out.
Then I'll be free.

MY LIFE CONTINUES BY
CHRISTOPHER PYLANT

After graduating from high school, I decided to go to a local Bible school. It gave me a good biblical foundation and opportunities to teach and preach. It was a great school, but I felt I needed more than that Bible school could provide. I applied and was accepted to Lee University in Cleveland, Tennessee. College was the fresh start I needed to overcome some preconceived ideas. I decided upon a major in Pastoral Ministry.

My first year at Lee was a thrilling experience. Being the first time I left home, it was a little unsettling; but after I arrived a sense of excitement and adventure rose up within me. It was not difficult to make acquaintances due to the warm and friendly atmosphere around campus. It was refreshing to know that they did not judge me on outward appearance. I could now be myself and feel accepted without pretense. There were so many activities and clubs to choose from in a social smorgasbord of opportunities for broadening my horizon. The teachers were interesting, stimulating, compassionate, and Spirit-filled. I excelled in both academics and social interaction. Over the course of the year, I took an interest in poetry and writing poems.

In my sophomore year, I got involved in a club called "Pioneers for Christ" and went on evangelistic outreaches with them to share my testimony. Another club that sparked my interest was "Ministry in Action." Again, having opportunities to share my testimony and ministering from the Bible was a great experience. In the pursuit of more social interaction, I rushed and was accepted into a Christian fraternity. Many more doors opened to share what God had done in my life.

In my last semester at Lee, a group of friends and I went to a campsite. There was a small mountain there and someone suggested climbing it. Naturally, I thought of my unsteady balance and weakness on the left side of my body. How could I possibly climb a mountain of any kind? A sense of courage suddenly arose within me as I faced the fear of my limitations. So with a little assistance from my friends, I put one foot in front of the other. Before I realized it, we were at the top! This was one of the highlights of my time at Lee. Proving to myself that perseverance, commitment, and hard work bring much success.

During my social bliss, I started to neglect my academic studies, allowing my grades to falter. My trying to burn the candle at both ends eventually caught up with me, causing my physical body to severely weaken. I had no choice but to withdraw from the university.

In the interim, before seeking a university to finish my education, I took a public speaking course in communications. The class helped to develop my strength and personality in oral presentations. Feeling a need to further improve my speaking abilities, especially because of my stutter, I began to see a speech therapist once a week. She taught me several techniques to help with anxiety.

My family and I eventually moved to Florida. I applied and was accepted to Southeastern University in Lakeland, Florida, changing my major to Practical Theology. My time there brought a new arena of ministry, which included my participation in a missions club, the preaching team, and prayer group.

My education at Southeastern gave me more understanding and insight into the Scriptures while preparing my mind and heart, and transforming my character for the work of ministry. I feel I gained a strong biblical and theological foundation to thrust me forward in the commission given to me by the Lord. The Holy Spirit has always been there to guide and strengthen me. Because of God's miracle healing on my body and mind, He has allowed me to graduate, with honors, earning my Bachelor of Science degree.

Today, I am pursing God's will for my life. I am humbled by His love and grace that has brought me this far. I still have challenges to face, but I know His strength will allow me to overcome all odds. I know if God can heal me, He can heal anybody—*for nothing is impossible with God* (see Luke 1:37).

THE PERFECT ENDING

For a long time Christopher continued to speak of things that I believed to be given to him by the Holy Spirit. One night, about five months after his release from the hospital, I was putting Christopher into his pajamas. He sat with Carole and me on our bed. Without warning, he began to speak of things neither Carole nor I were familiar with. Later, when sharing with friends from the church, we learned that the words he spoke were from the Bible.

When he began to speak, he was in a state of deep concentration. "Apple of His eye, apple of His eye, I'm the apple of His eye." He continued by saying, "The seed, the seed has to be planted." While tugging at his pajama shirt he repeated, "The seed has to be planted, to bring forth the bread."

While writing this manuscript, I referred to Christopher as God's promised seed, giving life to a dying generation. He is an heir to carry on our family's name. It now has been many years since his illness. Christopher has accomplished much, grown stronger in God's Word, and has had numerous opportunities to preach the gospel. Throughout the years, God confirmed what Christopher had spoken. However, He waited 26 years to give me revelation to this one.

I feel confident that Christopher was under the power of the Holy Spirit as he spoke—speaking prophetically of the call of God on his life. He was acknowledging that he was the apple of God's eye. By tugging on his pajama shirt, he was identifying himself as the seed that had been planted to bring forth the bread (preaching the gospel of Jesus Christ).

The Bible tells us that God's ways are not as our ways and His thoughts are not like ours (see Isa. 55:8-9). Indeed I learned this even more as I continued to work on this story. God protected His seed from being devoured by the enemy while it was being rooted in his mother's womb. Then, as the seed developed and came forth as a tender plant, Satan came again to kill him.

Before God granted us a miracle, He tested Carole's and my faith, allowing us time to grow in the knowledge of His Word so we could stand strong to defeat the enemy that had come to destroy our lives. I am humbled that God loves us so much that He gave the life of His only Son, Jesus Christ, that our son could live.

You have joined us in our most swirling and turbulent years. Yes, they were painful and difficult. However, we learned life's lessons that we never could have picked up in a book or by sitting in a classroom. As individuals, as a couple, as parents, as a family, and as Christians we have shared our thoughts and experiences. Our prayer is that this story will help build your faith and encourage you to lean on God even when nothing makes sense and all the reports are negative.

"Everything is possible for him who believes" (Mark 9:23 NIV).

Appendix A

CHRISTOPHER'S PUBLISHED POEMS

"SEIZE THE DAY"
by Christopher O'Neal Pylant

Breathing, existing, living,
Life is a mystery as well as a journey.
Quickly go the years.
We wish for more happiness then tears.
Time marches on.
Enjoy your life, for it is quickly fading.
Don't be afraid to take risks, pursue love,
and treasure family and friends.
Cause everything else is vanity in the end.
Take time to sing and feel your soul soar.
Learn to dance above your problems.
Always smile to brighten someone's day.
Drink in the moments that take your breath away.
Wrap yourself in awe, at the beauty of a sunset.
Slow down and smell the roses.
Life has a sweet nectar all its own.
Life is beautiful.
There is a rhythm to life.

If you listen closely, you will hear a song inside you.
A legacy awaits you, so dream.
Dream big!
Share your song with the world.
Don't be afraid to be different.
Your uniqueness is beautiful.
Be generous and kind to everybody.
Share the love you have with all.
Live each day as if it is your last.
I have said all this to say…
Seize the day!

"TIME"
by Christopher O'Neal Pylant

Time is the enemy of humanity.
Time is the one thing no one can control.
Time slips away without any remorse.
Time does not play favorites.
Young and old, rich and poor
Each future is held in the hands
of an unmerciful foe.
When you are young, there is no conception of time
How unaware we stumble upon the
numbers that will fill our days.
There is a time for everything.
A time to dance, a time to laugh, a time to love
Beware, time stands still for no one.
Time marches on and we must move with it.
No chance to breathe or slow down.
Make the most of the time you've been given.
Live life without regret.

Appendix B

DR. BEN CARSON

During the early stages of writing our story, I had a telephone conversation with Dr. Carson. He said to me, "When I first met you all, I was an unknown. The success we experienced with Christopher's case encouraged me to tackle other radical surgeries such as a hemispherectomy, a surgical procedure to remove half of the brain." He continued, "But don't forget, if it had not been for your tremendous faith in God, that He was going to heal your son, I would have never agreed to try anything more because it looked so hopeless." He stated that many lives had been changed because of this miraculous occurrence; not only changes in his life and work, but also in the life of a colleague who never believed in God at all.

In Dr. Carson's bestseller, *Think Big: Unleashing Your Potential for Excellence,* he writes about a doctor who was working with him as a neuro-oncologist. The young doctor said to him, "I've been an atheist for a long time, or maybe I just did not see any need for God. But the Christopher Pylant incident has changed my thinking. The faith of those parents and the result with their son has had a profound effect on me. There's got to be something to religion," he added, "in fact, more than this, honestly, this has made me a believer."

Several times during the first year of Christopher's recovery, this young doctor called to check on Christopher's progress. He would say, "Mr. Pylant, you know that man could have done nothing to help your son. You must thank the Man (God) upstairs." How beautiful it is to know how this miracle has affected so many lives. Not only did the Lord give us back our son, but also a non-believer came to acknowledge God.

Carole, a Jewish mother, received her Messiah. I, a backslidden Christian, rededicated my life to Jesus. A brilliant young doctor named Ben Carson recognized even more the awesome presence of God in his life and work, encouraging him to proceed with more radical surgical techniques.

I asked Dr. Carson if he could provide me statistics on the number of people who might have survived a brain stem astrosytoma stage four cancer, as Christopher had. His reply was, "To my knowledge, there is none," implying that Christopher is perhaps the lone survivor.

Victorious over death!

To God be the glory!

PROPHETIC WORDS SPOKEN OVER CHRISTOPHER, NEAL, AND CAROLE

FOR CHRISTOPHER AT AGE 5— NOVEMBER 14, 1985

- "You're a very special young man and it was ordained that you be born. It was not something people thought would happen. He chose Mommy and Daddy for you and He wants them to raise you and train you up for His purpose...."

- "You are going to walk with Him."

- "Someday you will talk into a microphone, telling a lot of people about Jesus. Many will be saved and some will even be healed."

- "God has given you a tender heart and a good mind."

- "My son, I've put a great and special call on your life. I'm calling you to be a Davidic man. You will have a heart like David and be a leader, a ruler, and a warrior for Me...."

- "No one shall have their hands on you because I have put your feet on the path. I've set this path for you so be strong and single-minded."

- "Do not be entangled with the world but be strong for Me."

- "You shall lead many into higher realms."

- "You shall have a special kind of wisdom."

- "You are God's man in a little boy's body."

- "Your heart cries a lot right now because your body has been so sick, but you won't feel that kind of pain for long. God feels pain for the world and so will you."

- "You are gentle and tender as you walk among the crowds, leading people in love."

- "I see you as a tugboat going through wavy water, but your Mommy and Daddy will make it smooth. There is a rope tied behind you and you are pulling a ship full of people."

- "Every cell will be made whole. Nothing will be lost."

- "Don't be discouraged by the way you have to walk. I haven't withdrawn from you. I'll remove the obstacles that are placed before you."

- "The enemy will come against you but I have prepared a shield. Move in boldness and have confidence. I'm going to open doors. I have prepared the way for you so step through."

For Neal:

- "There has been a cloud full of weariness and stress even though you're a man of faith. The Lord wants to speak peace over the tightness in your chest. Relax. Satan, you must loosen the bands around his heart! God wants to speak health and peace into your body and every fiber of your being—even in your back and head. There will be supernatural buoyancy. Lift Him up and the shackles will fall off!"

- "You think you are here for Chris. Wrong! God's going to move you into the prophetic and it will come soon with great excitement."

For Neal and Carole:

- "The Lord chooses and calls people to be perfect parents. You are to teach Chris what he needs to know about Jesus…and be a good example."

For Carole:

- "I heard you in the night time; your sobs, your cries. I heard the cries of your heart when you asked for a child and I gave you a baby. When the devil tried to rob him from you and you cried out, "God, I don't have enough faith," I gave you supernatural faith and surrounded you with faithful friends. I heard the cries of your heart. Now it is time for your tears to turn to joy. The time for deliverance has come!"

FOR THE PYLANT FAMILY:

- "The road won't be easy. There will be persecutions, trials, and testing, but I am compassionate. I desire to show you compassion. Hold out to the end and I will give you strength for the tasks I set before you."

ABOUT THE AUTHORS

NEAL PYLANT

Neal Pylant was born in Atlanta, Georgia, has worked in sales, owned and operated hair salons both in Maryland and Georgia, and worked with a Christian broadcasting network. He enjoys singing and writing. He has sung in church choirs and performed solos, both in churches and with a Gospel Jubilee group. Neal is now retired, having more time to devote to writing. He has two children, two grandsons, and currently lives with his wife, Carole, and their poodle, Angel, in Lakeland, Florida.

CHRISTOPHER PYLANT

Christopher Pylant was born in Towson, Maryland, graduated from Southeastern University with a Bachelor of Science degree in Practical Theology. He's an avid reader, writes poetry, and enjoys the arts. He has spoken in various churches, youth/college groups, and outreach ministries, and has done volunteer work with a Christian ministry where he resides in Lakeland, Florida.

For ministry or speaking engagements, contact at:

Website: www.atouchfromheaven.net
Email: chosenvessel23@tampabay.rr.com
PO Box 8740, Lakeland, FL 33806

IN THE RIGHT HANDS, THIS BOOK WILL CHANGE LIVES!

Most of the people who need this message will not be looking for this book. To change their lives, you need to put a copy of this book in their hands.

> *But others (seeds) fell into good ground, and brought forth fruit, some a hundred-fold, some sixty-fold, some thirty-fold* (Matthew 13:8).

Our ministry is constantly seeking methods to find the good ground, the people who need this anointed message to change their lives. Will you help us reach these people?

> *Remember this—a farmer who plants only a few seeds will get a small crop. But the one who plants generously will get a generous crop* (2 Corinthians 9:6).

EXTEND THIS MINISTRY BY SOWING
3 BOOKS, 5 BOOKS, 10 BOOKS, **OR MORE TODAY,**
AND BECOME A LIFE CHANGER!

Thank you,

Don Nori Sr.

Don Nori Sr., Founder
Destiny Image
Since 1982